Harrisburg's Camelback Bridge in 1880. It was designed by Theodore Burr, who was responsible for four other substantial covered bridges which spanned the Susquehanna. The two sections of this bridge, which crossed Hargest (now City) Island, were 2,876 feet long and 40 feet wide. To give a sense of the scale of the Camelback Bridge, the longest extant covered bridge in Pennsylvania today is the 270 foot long 15 foot 6 inch wide Academia Bridge in Juniata County.

The contract for construction of the Camelback Bridge was signed in 1812 and the structure was completed in 1817, at a cost of $192,138. The eastern portion of the bridge was washed away in the flood of 1846 and reconstructed in 1847. However, the rebuilt eastern section burned in 1867 and was replaced by a conventional covered bridge. The western section of the Camelback Bridge survived until 1903, when both sections of the bridge were demolished.

Photo: J. Horace McFarland, from the collection of The State Archives of Pennsylvania

Cover: Packsaddle Bridge (1870) across Brush Creek, Somerset County. Photo: Isaac Geib, Grant Heilman Photography, Lititz, Pennsylvania.

The Covered Bridges of Pennsylvania

A Guide

Susan M. Zacher

▲▲▲▲▲▲▲▲▲▲▲▲▲▲▲▲▲▲▲▲▲▲▲▲▲▲▲▲▲▲▲▲▲▲▲▲▲▲

SECOND EDITION

Commonwealth of Pennsylvania
Pennsylvania Historical
and Museum Commission
Harrisburg, 1994

THE PENNSYLVANIA HISTORICAL AND MUSEUM COMMISSION

Robert P. Casey
GOVERNOR

Kurt D. Zwikl
CHAIRMAN

COMMISSIONERS

Frank S. Beal

Michael E. Bortner, *Senator*

Bernard J. Dombrowski

Robert H. Fowler, Sr.

Constance Glott-Maine

Ann N. Greene

William F. Heefner

Edwin G. Holl, *Senator*

Stephen R. Maitland, *Representative*

LeRoy Patrick

James R. Roebuck, *Representative*

Anna Rotz

Donald M. Carroll, Jr., *Ex Officio*
Secretary of Education

Brent D. Glass
EXECUTIVE DIRECTOR

Second Edition 1994
Copyright © 1982, 1994 Commonwealth of Pennsylvania
ISBN 0-89271-054-3

Part of the cost of the preparation of this publication was funded by a survey and planning grant congressionally authorized by the National Preservation Act of 1966, administered by the U.S. Department of the Interior, National Park Service.

CONTENTS

INTRODUCTION

The covered bridge is an important historic structure in Pennsylvania. Not only does Pennsylvania, with 215, have the most covered bridges today, it probably had the most during the height of the covered-bridge period, 1830 to 1880. Estimates have been made that Pennsylvania once had at least fifteen-hundred covered bridges. In fact, Pennsylvania had the first covered bridge to be built in the United States and the prototypes of most of the major truss designs.

The first covered bridge was located in Philadelphia over the Schuylkill River; it was built in 1800 by Timothy Palmer, a master carpenter from Newburyport, Massachusetts. From the completion of this first bridge, the age of the covered bridge was upon Pennsylvania. Not only were the truss designs of Burr and others tested in Pennsylvania, carpenters throughout the state were adapting them to the local problem of crossing the numerous small streams and creeks.

The covered bridge is also an important development in the history of bridge building. The early stone-arch bridges were really practical only on small streams, and only in areas with an abundance of good building stone. The greatest achievement in the building of the stone bridge in Pennsylvania can be seen in the Rockville Bridge over the Susquehanna River, built by the Pennsylvania Railroad with a quarter-million tons of stone. In most places, however, the covered bridge provided the transition from the stone to the cast-iron bridge.

Since the heyday of the covered bridge, it has been rapidly disappearing through neglect, flood, arson and progress. Prior to the Agnes Flood of 1972, Pennsylvania had 271 covered bridges spread across forty-one of its sixty-seven counties. At the time of preparation for the second edition of this guide, Pennsylvania has 215 covered bridges standing in thirty-seven counties. Since the last printing of this guide in 1986, the state has lost an additional six wooden spans to arson, collapse and highway projects. Several others have been damaged and their preservation is not assured. However, state, county and local governments are now working more closely with the Pennsylvania Historical and Museum Commission to find solutions that are an alternative to demolition. This guide book was compiled from the results of a survey of Pennsylvania covered bridges conducted by the Pennsylvania Historical and Museum Commission, Bureau for Historic Preservation, in 1979-1980, and has been updated with help from government agencies and concerned citizens.

The intent of this survey was to determine how many wooden spans remained and then to nominate all the eligible covered bridges to the National Register of Historic Places. The National Register is a list of the nation's historic resources considered worthy of preservation. The National Register is maintained by the United States Department of the Interior. To be listed on the National Register a resource must be at least fifty years old and possess architectural or historical significance.

In the past several years there has been an increased interest in the preservation of the covered bridges of Pennsylvania. The maintenance of these wooden bridges has often been viewed as more expensive than their replacement with a new bridge. Many in Pennsylvania have begun to recognize the significance of our covered bridges and their importance to the tourist industry. In 1991 the Pennsylvania Department of Transportation, with the help of many governmental and municipal agencies, preservation organizations, and concerned citizens, completed a statewide assessment of Pennsylvania's covered bridges. This assessment was a combination of resurvey and the evaluation of the condition of each bridge and the cost of its rehabilitation and maintenance. As a result of this survey new information concerning the length of each bridge, construction dates and builders was added to this publication.

Key to the Use of This Guide Book

Within each region, the bridges are divided by county. All the historic bridges, defined as more than fifty years old, have been included. The listing for each bridge includes its location, the stream it crosses, the truss type, the span length and width of the bridge, and its condition. When known, the builder and year of construction have been included. Not all counties kept records of the builders or the years of construction of their bridges; therefore, our records are incomplete in these areas. There has been no attempt to record or mention by name the many covered bridges which once existed in each of the counties.

To find the bridges, use a standard highway map to reach the general location. Most counties have their roads marked with the township route or state route placed on small rectangular metal signs at each intersection. Included in the index are the UTM (Universal Transverse Mercator, the metric replacement for longitude and latitude) points for each bridge, as presented on the United States Geological Survey maps.

TRUSS TYPES

A bridge is an object designed to span a gap and support itself as well as the crossing load. The bridge truss is a framework of beams which support each other and remain rigid. The basis of all truss systems is the triangle, the only geometric form which cannot be distorted under load.

THE KINGPOST TRUSS

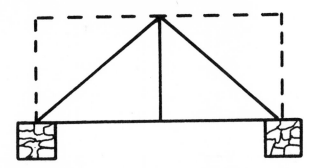

This is the oldest and simplest truss, basically a triangle with reinforcing timbers. Bridges using this truss are seldom over thirty-five feet in length. Pennsylvania's shortest kingpost-truss bridges are only twenty-four feet (Krepp's Bridge and Devil's Den Bridge, Washington County). The longest bridge of this type uses several kingpost trusses for a total length of seventy-five feet (Carman Bridge, Erie County). Pennsylvania has a total of twenty-six kingpost-truss bridges today.

THE QUEENPOST TRUSS

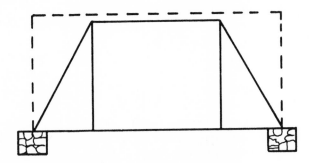

This truss uses a truncated triangle with supporting posts at each end. The crosspiece, which must be separate from the highest sidewall timbers, permits greater bridge length, usually sixty to seventy feet. Pennsylvania has thirty-five extant queenpost-truss bridges.

THE BURR TRUSS

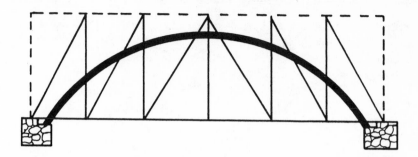

Theodore Burr, of Torringford, Connecticut, patented a wooden-span trussing system in 1804. The Burr arch truss, as it became known, combined great reinforced arches with multiple kingpost trusses. These arches tie directly into the bridge's abutments, permitting wider streams and rivers to be spanned. Most Burr arch-truss bridges are one hundred feet or more in length. Pennsylvania has 124 remaining Burr arch-truss covered bridges. The shortest Burr-arch bridge is sixty feet (Cupperts Bridge, Bedford County) and the longest is 185 feet (Rupert Bridge, Columbia County). These bridges are most prevalent in the Susquehanna River watershed, probably due to the influence of Theodore Burr himself. Burr built some of his earliest and largest bridges in this area of Pennsylvania.

THE TOWN TRUSS

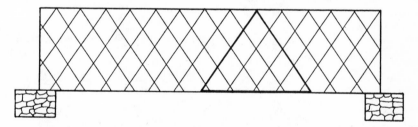

The Town truss, often called the lattice truss, was designed and patented by Ithiel Town, an architect from New Haven, Connecticut, in 1820. This truss consists of a lattice of crossing beams at an angle of forty-five to sixty degrees, connected by wooden pins. The Town truss proved so strong and easy to build that it was later used and adapted for railroad bridges of wood and cast iron. This truss had scattered popularity in Pennsylvania, seeing its greatest use in Bucks County. Pennsylvania's shortest Town-truss bridge is only thirty-five feet (Dice's Bridge, Indiana County) and the longest is 200 feet (Martin's Mill Bridge, Franklin County). The Martin's Mill Bridge is also the longest remaining covered bridge in Pennsylvania. There are seventeen Town-truss bridges in Pennsylvania.

THE HOWE TRUSS

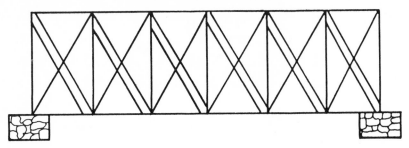

The Howe truss, patented by Massachusetts's William Howe in 1840, substitutes iron rods for some of the wooden tension members. This substitution made shipping and prefabricating possible and also allowed for adjustment of the bridge. Pennsylvania has only four Howe-truss covered bridges.

THE WARREN TRUSS

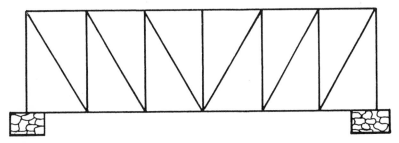

Patented by two Englishmen, James Warren and T. W. Morzani in 1838, the Warren truss uses lightweight timbers placed in the form of a W. Pennsylvania has two examples of the double Warren system, which adds a second set of diagonals.

THE SMITH TRUSS

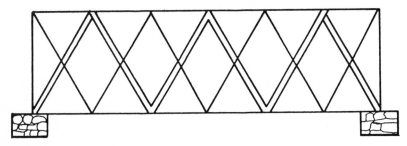

The unusual Smith truss was designed and patented by Robert J. Smith of Ohio. He designed four versions of this trussing system, none of which ever became extremely popular. Pennsylvania has one example of the Smith truss (Kidds Mill Bridge, Mercer County).

Southwest

R·E·G·I·O·N

The southwest region of Pennsylvania has sixty-three remaining covered bridges. The concentration of these wooden spans is in the lower border counties. The Ohio River and the western Susquehanna River watersheds drain this area of Pennsylvania.

Washington and Green counties have the largest remaining collection of queenpost- and kingpost-truss bridges in the state. Most of the bridges are small and unadorned and were built by local carpenters to serve the transportation needs of local communities and farms. Bedford and Somerset County bridges show a regional use of open sidewalls, which leave the trussing system open to view.

Three of Pennsylvania's Town-truss bridges are located in Indiana County, as well as two of the four remaining Howe-truss bridges.

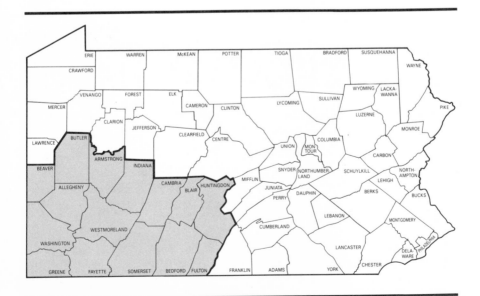

1

Felton's Mill Bridge

Location: On S.R. 2029 west of Jackson Mills and south of the Pennsylvania Turnpike in East Providence Township.

Stream: Brush Creek
Ownership: Private
Truss type: Burr
Length: 105 ft.

Width: 12 ft. 6 in.
Builder: Mullins, W. S.
Year: 1892
Condition: Fair

Located near Felton's Mill, this open-sidewall bridge has a moderately pitched gable roof with wide overhangs. It is currently closed to traffic.

Heirline Bridge

Location: On S.R. 4007 northwest of Manns Choice and the Pennsylvania Turnpike in Harrison and Napier townships.

Stream: Juniata River
Ownership: State
Truss type: Burr
Length: 136 ft.

Width: 8 ft. 10 in.
Builder: Unknown
Year: 1902
Condition: Good

This Burr arch-truss bridge has high sidewalls leaving narrow window rows under the eaves. Heirline is the longest remaining covered bridge in Bedford County.

Claycomb, Reynoldsdale Bridge

Location: In Old Bedford Village off U.S. 220, 2 miles north of Bedford. Originally this bridge was located on S.R. 4015 in Reynoldsdale.

Stream: Raystown Branch, Juniata
River
Ownership: Private
Truss type: Burr
Length: 126 ft.

Width: 13 ft. 10 in.
Builder: Unknown
Year: 1880
Condition: Excellent

The Claycomb, Reynoldsdale Bridge was moved to Old Bedford Village in 1975. A covered walkway was added to the bridge at that time, similar to the Lawrence L. Knoebel Bridge in Columbia County.

Hall's Mill Bridge

Location: On township route 528 just east of Yellow Creek in Hopewell Township.

Stream: Yellow Creek
Ownership: County
Truss type: Burr
Length: 91 ft.

Width: 12 ft. 6 in.
Builder: Unknown
Year: 1872
Condition: Fair

This shallow gable-roofed bridge has low sidewalls leaving the trussing system open. Foundations of the old Hall's Mill can be seen at the west end of the bridge.

Claycomb, Reynoldsdale Bridge

Dr. Knisley Bridge

Location: Off S.R. 4013, 2.5 miles northeast of Ryot near the junction with route 96 in West St. Clair Township.

Stream: Dunnings Creek
Ownership: Private
Truss type: Burr
Length: 80 ft.

Width: 12 ft. 7 in.
Builder: Unknown
Year: 1867
Condition: Good

The low sidewalls of this bridge leave a clear view of the trussing system, a feature common in Bedford County covered bridges.

Ryot Bridge

Location: On township route 559 north of Spring Meadow in West St. Clair Township.

Stream: Dunnings Creek	**Width:** 12 ft.
Ownership: County	**Builder:** Unknown
Truss type: Burr	**Year:** 1868
Length: 83 ft.	**Condition:** Good

The Ryot Bridge has high Burr-arch trusses extending almost to eave level and a low-pitched gable roof, as well as low interior sidewalls. All of Bedford County covered bridges have interior sidewalls.

Cupperts, New Paris Bridge

Location: On private land 1 mile north of New Paris in Napier Township.

Stream: Dunnings Creek	**Width:** 12 ft.
Ownership: Private	**Builder:** Unknown
Truss type: Burr	**Year:** Unknown
Length: 60 ft.	**Condition:** Poor

This unusual bridge has very low Burr-arch trusses with low sidewalls curving to cover the arches. The upper trussing is tied by horizontal rods the length of the bridge. It also does not have portals—only squared pillars support the gabled roof.

Raystown Bridge

McDaniels Bridge

Raystown, Diehl's Bridge

Location: On township route 418 just south of the Pennsylvania Turnpike in Harrison Township.

Stream: Raystown Branch, Juniata River
Ownership: County
Truss type: Burr
Length: 88 ft. 4 in.

Width: 12 ft. 10 in.
Builder: Unknown
Year: 1892
Condition: Good

The Diehl's Bridge, with its high Burr-arch trusses and low sidewalls, can be seen from the Pennsylvania Turnpike.

McDaniels Bridge

Location: Was located west of Felton's Mill Covered Bridge, spanning East and West Providence townships.

Stream: Brush Creek
Ownership: County
Truss type: Burr
Length: 110 ft.

Width: 20 ft.
Builder: Unknown
Year: 1873

The McDaniels Bridge was similar in style to the Ryot Bridge. This bridge was destroyed by fire.

Fischtner Bridge

Location: On private land just south of Palo Alto in Londonderry Township.

Stream: Gladdens Run	**Width:** 13 ft.
Ownership: Private	**Builder:** Unknown
Truss type: Kingpost	**Year:** 1880
Length: 56 ft.	**Condition:** Good

This bridge is currently used for access to private land and has an unusual trussing system for Bedford County. The kingpost truss system is usually used for bridges under thirty-five feet; however as shown in the Fischtner Bridge, this practice is not always followed.

Bowser, Osterburg Bridge

Location: On township route 575 northwest of Osterburg in East St. Clair Township.

Stream: Bobs Creek	**Width:** 12 ft. 4 in.
Ownership: Private	**Builder:** Unknown
Truss type: Burr	**Year:** 1890
Length: 90 ft.	**Condition:** Good

This bridge is similar to other open-sided covered bridges throughout the county and has the horizontal bracing seen in the New Paris Bridge.

Snooks Bridge

Location: On township route 578 north of Spring Meadow in East St. Clair Township.

Stream: Dunnings Creek	**Width:** 7 ft. 8 in.
Ownership: County	**Builder:** Unknown
Truss type: Burr	**Year:** 1880
Length: 82 ft.	**Condition:** Excellent

The Snooks Bridge has high sidewalls blocking an exterior view of the trussing system and leaving window openings under the eaves. This bridge has been braced with steel pillars under the arches and cross bracing under the roof.

Colvin or Calvin Bridge

Location: On township route 443 northwest of Shawnee State Park in Napier Township.

Stream: Shawnee Creek	**Width:** 12 ft. 3 in.
Ownership: County	**Builder:** Unknown
Truss type: Kingpost	**Year:** 1880
Length: 66 ft.	**Condition:** Good

This unusual bridge has completely open sidewalls, the only bridge of its type in Pennsylvania. Its multiple kingpost trusses are tied by horizontal beams at their mid-points. The shallow gable roof has triangular portal extensions on only one side; these may have been present on all four sides originally.

Colvin Bridge

Jackson's Mill Bridge

Location: On township route 412 in Jackson Mills in East Providence Township.

Stream: Brush Creek
Ownership: County
Truss type: Burr
Length: 91 ft.

Width: 15 ft.
Builder: Karns Rohm
Year: 1889
Condition: Poor

Jackson's Mill Bridge is similar in style to the Ryot and McDaniels bridges with its Burr trusses, high sidewalls, eave-level windows and interior walls. It is also attributed to builders A. D. Bottomfield and Joe Pee in 1875.

Hewitt Bridge

Location: On township route 305 in Hewitt, Southampton Township.

Stream: Town Creek
Ownership: County
Truss type: Burr
Length: 88 ft.

Width: 13 ft. 10 in.
Builder: Unknown
Year: 1880
Condition: Excellent

This medium-gable-roofed bridge has high vertical-plank sidewalls, cut-stone abutments and low interior walls, a very plain but attractive bridge.

GREENE COUNTY

(See also Washington/Greene Counties)

Carmichaels Bridge

Location: On township route 684, Carmichaels.

Stream: Muddy Creek
Ownership: County
Truss type: Queenpost
Length: 64 ft.

Width: 15 ft.
Builder: Unknown
Year: 1889
Condition: Good

Carmichaels Bridge has vertical, board-and-batten siding, a gable roof covered with raised-seam tin and cut-stone abutments.

Carmichaels Bridge

King Bridge

Shriver Bridge

Location: On township route 454 south of Rogersville in Center Township.

Stream: Hargus Creek	**Width:** 15 ft.
Ownership: County	**Builder:** Unknown
Truss type: Queenpost	**Year:** 1900
Length: 40 ft.	**Condition:** Good

The Shriver Bridge is identical in styling to other Greene County covered bridges, but has two large windows cut into each sidewall.

King Bridge

Location: On township route 371 south of Kuhntown in Wayne Township.

Stream: Hoover Creek	**Width:** 15 ft.
Ownership: County	**Builder:** Unknown
Truss type: Queenpost	**Year:** Unknown
Length: 46 ft. 6 in.	**Condition:** Good

This rustic bridge has unpainted vertical-plank siding and a tin-covered gable roof. Most of Greene County's covered bridges use the queenpost and kingpost truss systems and were probably built by local carpenters.

Lippincott Bridge

Location: On township route 568 northwest of Lippincott in Morgan Township.

Stream: Ruff Creek	**Width:** 15 ft.
Ownership: County	**Builder:** Unknown
Truss type: Kingpost	**Year:** 1943
Length: 27 ft. 8 in.	**Condition:** Good

This unusual bridge has narrow, horizontal siding and narrow windows under the eaves. Built in 1943 because of a shortage of steel during the war, this bridge continues to serve the local traffic.

Red, Neils Bridge

Location: Was located between Garards Fort and Willow Tree in Greene Township.

Stream: Whiteley Creek	**Width:** 15 ft.
Ownership: State	**Builder:** Unknown
Truss type: Burr	**Year:** 1900
Length: 86 ft.	

The Red, Neils Bridge had rough vertical-plank siding, and a tin-covered gable roof. This was one of the two Burr arch-truss bridges in Greene County. The other Burr bridge is located between Green and Washington counties. The Red, Neils Bridge was destroyed by fire.

Scott Bridge

Scott Bridge

Location: On township route 424 southeast of Rutan in Center Township.

Stream: Ten Mile Creek
Ownership: County
Truss type: Queenpost
Length: 41 ft.

Width: 15 ft.
Builder: William Lang
Year: 1885
Condition: Fair

The Scott Bridge has vertical-plank siding and a tin-covered gable roof. Greene County has the third largest number of queenpost-truss covered bridges remaining in Pennsylvania.

Grimes Bridge

Grimes Bridge

Location: On township route 546 southeast of Ruff Creek in Washington Township.

Stream: Ruff Creek
Ownership: County
Truss type: Kingpost
Length: 31 ft. 8 in.

Width: 15 ft.
Builder: Unknown
Year: 1888
Condition: Fair

Grimes Bridge has vertical-plank siding, a gable roof covered with raised-seam tin, and cut-stone abutments.

Neddie Woods Bridge

White Bridge

Location: On township route 604 west of Garards Fort in Greene Township.

Stream: Whiteley Creek
Ownership: County
Truss type: Queenpost
Length: 66 ft. 6 in.

Width: 15 ft.
Builder: Unknown
Year: 1919
Condition: Good

White Bridge is the longest of the queenpost bridges in Greene County. It has high, narrow, vertical siding and a tin-covered gable roof.

Neddie Woods Bridge

Location: On township route 487 north of Oak Forest in Center Township.

Stream: Pursley Creek
Ownership: County
Truss type: Queenpost
Length: 40 ft.

Width: 15 ft.
Builder: Lisbon Scott
Year: 1882
Condition: Good

This bridge was named for Edward (Ned or Neddie) W. Wood, a Civil War veteran who owned the land on which it was built. It is also the oldest bridge in the county and identical in style with the other remaining bridges.

St. Mary's, Shade Gap Bridge

Location: On township route 358 south of Orbisonia in Cromwell Township.

Stream: Shade Creek
Ownership: County
Truss type: Howe
Length: 65 ft. 4 in.

Width: 17 ft. 6 in.
Builder: Unknown
Year: 1889
Condition: Excellent

The St. Mary's Bridge has open sidewalls exposing the trussing, similar to Bedford County covered bridges. This bridge is one of four Howe-truss bridges remaining in Pennsylvania and the last covered bridge in this county.

St. Mary's Bridge

Dice's, Trussal Bridge

Location: On township route 406 between Willet and Davis in Washington Township.

Stream: Plum Creek
Ownership: County
Truss type: Town
Length: 35 ft.

Width: 15 ft.
Builder: Unknown
Year: 1870
Condition: Good

One of the seventeen Town-truss bridges in Pennsylvania, the Trussal Bridge has vertical siding and a gable roof. Harmon's Bridge can be seen up the valley from this bridge.

Dice's, Trussal Bridge

Harmon's Bridge

Location: On township route 408 between Willet and Davis in Washington Township.

Stream: Plum Creek
Ownership: County
Truss type: Town
Length: 41 ft.

Width: 15 ft.
Builder: John R. Carnahan
Year: 1910
Condition: Good

Harmon's Bridge is identical in styling to the Trussal Bridge, with its vertical siding, gable roof and triangular portals.

Kintersburg Bridge

Location: On township route 612 near Kintersburg, Rayne Township.

Stream: Crooked Creek
Ownership: County
Truss type: Howe
Length: 62 ft.

Width: 15 ft.
Builder: J. S. Fleming
Year: 1877
Condition: Fair

This bridge has been by-passed but can still be crossed on foot. The Kintersburg Bridge is the smallest of Pennsylvania's four Howe-truss bridges.

Kintersburg Bridge

Thomas Ford Bridge

Location: On township route 414 northeast of Shelocta in Armstrong Township.

Stream: Crooked Creek
Ownership: County
Truss type: Town
Length: 52 ft.

Width: 15 ft.
Builder: Amos Thomas
Year: 1879
Condition: Good

The Thomas Bridge is the longest of the Indiana County Town-truss bridges. Pennsylvania has only seventeen Town-truss covered bridges.

Beechdale, Burkholder Bridge

Location: On township route 548 southwest of Berlin in Brothers Valley Township.

Stream: Buffalo Creek
Ownership: County
Truss type: Burr
Length: 52 ft.

Width: 12 ft.
Builder: Unknown
Year: 1870
Condition: Good

This short bridge has a very shallow Burr arch and low vertical-plank sidewalls, leaving much of the trussing open to view. Its gable roof is tin covered.

Beechdale, Burkholder Bridge

Packsaddle Bridge

Location: On township route 407 northwest of Fairhope in Fairhope Township.

Stream: Brush Creek
Ownership: County
Truss type: Kingpost
Length: 47 ft.

Width: 14 ft.
Builder: Unknown
Year: 1870
Condition: Excellent

The Packsaddle Bridge has full vertical-plank siding and large cut-stone abutments.

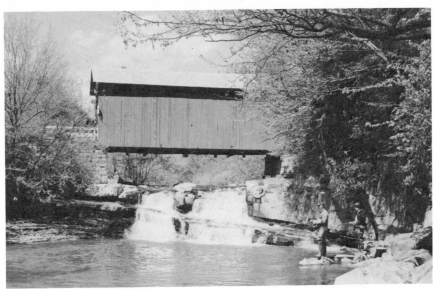

Packsaddle Bridge

Barronvale Bridge

Location: On township route 501 northwest of New Lexington in Middlecreek
Township.

Stream: Laurel Hill Creek **Width:** 13 ft. 10 in.
Ownership: Private **Builder:** Cassimer Cramer
Truss type: Burr **Year:** 1902
Length: 162 ft. 3 in. **Condition:** Fair

This is the longest covered bridge remaining in Somerset County. Its low Burr-
arch trussing is protected by vertical-plank half sidewalls. Its portal design is
identical to King's Bridge.

Walter's Mill Bridge

Location: 400 ft. west of Rt. 985, Somerset Historical Center grounds in Somerset Township.

Stream: Haupts Run **Width:** 12 ft.
Ownership: State **Builder:** Christian Ankeny
Truss type: Burr **Year:** 1830
Length: 60 ft. **Condition:** Fair

The Walter's Mill Bridge was originally located across Coxes Creek four miles
south of Somerset. One of the oldest in the state, this bridge has vertical-plank
siding and a tin-covered gable roof.

Barronvale Bridge

Walter's Mill Bridge

King's Bridge

Location: On route 653 west of New Lexington in Middlecreek Township.

Stream: Laurel Hill Creek
Ownership: Private
Truss type: Burr
Length: 127 ft. 4 in.

Width: 12 ft. 4 in.
Builder: Unknown
Year: 1906
Condition: Fair

Set on large cut-stone abutments, the King's Bridge has an asbestos-covered gable roof. Its sidewalls are made up of vertical planking with a panel of windows under the eaves.

Glessner Bridge

Location: On township route 565 northwest of Shanksville in Stony Creek Township.

Stream: Stony Creek
Ownership: County
Truss type: Kingpost
Length: 90 ft.

Width: 12 ft.
Builder: Tobias Glessner
Year: 1881
Condition: Good

This long multiple kingpost-truss bridge has a tin-covered gable roof, vertical-plank siding and a window panel under the eaves. Its portals have inside walls of vertical planking.

King's Bridge

Glessner Bridge

New Baltimore Bridge

New Baltimore Bridge

Location: On township route 812 east of New Baltimore in Allegheny Township.

Stream: Raystown Branch, Juniata River
Ownership: County
Truss type: Kingpost
Length: 86 ft. 6 in.

Width: 12 ft.
Builder: Unknown
Year: 1879
Condition: Good

The New Baltimore Bridge has a gable roof and full vertical-plank sidewalls. The portal design is similar in style to the Trostletown and Shaffer's bridges.

Trostletown Bridge

Location: On township route 666 southwest of Kantner in Quemahoning Township.

Stream: Stony Creek
Ownership: Private
Truss type: Kingpost
Length: 104 ft.

Width: 12 ft. 6 in.
Builder: Unknown
Year: 1845
Condition: Good

This multiple kingpost-truss bridge was restored in 1965 by the Stoystown Lions Club. The gable roof is covered with asbestos shingles.

Shaffer's Bridge

Location: On township route 634 north of Thomas Mills in Conemaugh Township.

Stream: Bens Creek
Ownership: County
Truss type: Burr
Length: 56 ft.

Width: 13 ft. 2 in.
Builder: Unknown
Year: 1877
Condition: Good

This low Burr arch-truss bridge has a gable roof covered with wooden shingles. Its sidewalls have vertical-plank siding, which only reaches to the top of the arches or halfway.

Lower Humbert Bridge

Location: On township route 312 north of Ursina in Lower Turkeyfoot Township.

Stream: Laurel Hill Creek
Ownership: County
Truss type: Burr
Length: 126 ft. 6 in.

Width: 12 ft. 4 in.
Builder: Unknown
Year: 1891
Condition: Good

The Lower Humbert Bridge is identical in styling to the majority of the remaining Somerset County covered bridges, with its half, vertical-plank siding, gable roof and portals. This bridge also has horizontal-plank inside walls.

WASHINGTON/GREENE COUNTIES

Davis, Horn, Overholtzer Bridge

Location: On township route 325 southeast of Zollarsville between West Bethlehem Township, Washington County, and Morgan Township, Greene County.

Stream: Ten Mile Creek
Ownership: Two counties
Truss type: Burr
Length: 87 ft.

Width: 14 ft. 3 in.
Builder: Unknown
Year: 1889
Condition: Fair

The present bridge replaced an earlier covered bridge c. 1838, which was destroyed by flood in 1888. Davis Bridge has vertical siding. This siding is cut to cover the Burr truss as it extends to the roof line.

Davis Bridge

(See also Washington/Greene Counties)

Sprowl's Bridge

Location: On township route 450 southwest of East Finley in East Finley Township.

Stream: Rocky Run
Ownership: County
Truss type: Kingpost
Length: 27 ft. 6 in.

Width: 12 ft. 7 in.
Builder: Unknown
Year: 1875
Condition: Good

The Sprowl's Bridge has vertical siding and a tin-covered gable roof. Square windows are cut into the sidewalls.

Bailey Bridge

Location: On township route 686 southeast of Amity in Amwell Township.

Stream: Ten Mile Creek
Ownership: County
Truss type: Burr
Length: 66 ft.

Width: 15 ft.
Builder: Bailey Brothers
Year: 1889
Condition: Good

The Bailey Bridge has vertical siding, a tin-covered gable roof and two windows piercing each sidewall. The cut-stone abutments and span are now supported by steel beams and a mid-stream concrete pier.

Bailey Bridge

Brownlee, Scott Bridge

Location: On township route 414 northeast of East Finley in East Finley Township.

Stream: Templeton Fork of Wheeling Creek
Ownership: County
Truss type: Kingpost
Length: 31 ft. 6 in.

Width: 11 ft. 7 in.
Builder: Unknown
Year: Unknown
Condition: Fair

This small bridge has rough vertical-plank siding.

Crawford Bridge

Location: On township route 307 south of Good Intent in West Finley Township.

Stream: Robinson Fork of Wheeling Creek
Ownership: County
Truss type: Queenpost
Length: 39 ft.

Width: 11 ft. 7 in.
Builder: Unknown
Year: Unknown
Condition: Good

The Crawford Bridge has high sidewalls of vertical planks and a tin-covered gable roof.

Danley Bridge

Location: On township route 379 north of Good Intent in West Finley Township.

Stream: Robinson Fork of Wheeling Creek
Ownership: County
Truss type: Queenpost
Length: 39 ft.

Width: 11 ft. 10 in.
Builder: Unknown
Year: Unknown
Condition: Good

A typical Washington County covered bridge, the Danley Bridge also has vertical-plank siding and a tin-covered gable roof. Like most of the county's covered bridges, it has a plain, boxlike appearance. It is thought that these bridges were the work of local carpenters.

Day Bridge

Location: On township route 339 east of Sparta in Morris Township.

Stream: Short Creek
Ownership: County
Truss type: Queenpost
Length: 36 ft. 6 in.

Width: 12 ft.
Builder: Unknown
Year: c. 1875
Condition: Good

A typical Washington County covered bridge, the Day Bridge abutments have been reinforced with concrete.

Devil's Den, McClurg Bridge

Location: Hanover Township Park off S.R. 4004.

Stream: Unnamed run
Ownership: County
Truss type: Kingpost
Length: 24 ft.

Width: 12 ft. 3 in.
Builder: Unknown
Year: Unknown
Condition: Good

The McClurg Bridge has vertical-plank sidewalls pierced on each side by four windows. It was moved to the park from Kings Creek.

Devil's Den, McClurg Bridge

Ebenezer Bridge

Location: Off S.R. 1087 in Mingo Creek County Park, Nottingham Township.

Stream: South Fork of Maple Creek
Ownership: County
Truss type: Queenpost
Length: 32 ft.

Width: 15 ft.
Builder: Unknown
Year: Unknown
Condition: Good

The Ebenezer Bridge was moved to Mingo Creek Park in 1977 and placed on the abutments of an earlier bridge. It has been altered but makes a nice addition to the park.

Erskine Bridge

Location: On township route 314 northwest of Kimmins School in West Finley Township.

Stream: Middle Wheeling Creek   **Width:** 11 ft. 8 in.
Ownership: County   **Builder:** William Gordon
Truss type: Queenpost   **Year:** 1845
Length: 39 ft. 6 in.   **Condition:** Good

The Erskine Bridge is the earliest-known bridge remaining in Washington County and is of the typical Washington County styling.

Henry Bridge

Location: On township route 822 east of Henry in Nottingham Township.

Stream: Mingo Creek   **Width:** 12 ft. 4 in.
Ownership: County   **Builder:** Unknown
Truss type: Queenpost   **Year:** c. 1881
Length: 36 ft.   **Condition:** Good

The Henry Bridge has vertical siding and a tin-covered gable roof, and the sidewalls are pierced by two square windows. The cut-stone abutments are braced by concrete supports.

Hughes Bridge

Location: On S.R. 2020 northwest of Ten Mile in Amwell Township.

Stream: Ten Mile Creek   **Width:** 12 ft. 4 in.
Ownership: Township   **Builder:** Unknown
Truss type: Queenpost   **Year:** 1889
Length: 55 ft. 6 in.   **Condition:** Fair

This bridge spans the backwater of the diverted Ten Mile Creek and is no longer used for traffic. The Hughes Bridge has vertical siding, with four windows on each side, and a tin-covered gable roof.

Jackson's Mill Bridge

Location: On township route 853 south of Boyd in Hanover Township.

Stream: Kings Creek   **Width:** 14 ft.
Ownership: County   **Builder:** Unknown
Truss type: Queenpost   **Year:** Unknown
Length: 35 ft.   **Condition:** Fair

A petition was filed for a bridge to be built at this site in 1865; however, this may be a later bridge. In many counties bridge records were not kept; this is the case in Washington County.

Jackson's Mill Bridge

Krepps Bridge

Location: On township route 799 south of Cherry Valley in Pleasant Township.

Stream: Cherry Creek
Ownership: County
Truss type: Kingpost
Length: 24 ft.

Width: 13 ft. 3 in.
Builder: Unknown
Year: Unknown
Condition: Fair

A typical Washington County bridge, the Krepps Bridge has been braced with wooden supports.

Leatherman Bridge

Location: On township route 449 northwest of Cokesburg in North Bethlehem Township.

Stream: South Branch of Pigeon
Creek
Ownership: County
Truss type: Queenpost
Length: 36 ft.

Width: 12 ft.
Builder: Unknown
Year: Unknown
Condition: Good

Leatherman Bridge has vertical-plank siding and a tin-covered gable roof.

Lyle Bridge

Location: On township route 861 southeast of Five Points in Hanover Township.

Stream: Brush Run
Ownership: County
Truss type: Queenpost
Length: 39 ft.

Width: 12 ft.
Builder: Unknown
Year: Unknown
Condition: Good

The Lyle Bridge is of typical Washington County design.

Longdon L. Miller Bridge

Location: On S.R. 2020 south of Liberty in West Finley Township.

Stream: Templeton Fork of Wheeling Creek
Ownership: County
Truss type: Queenpost
Length: 67 ft. 6 in.

Width: 11 ft. 10 in.
Builder: Unknown
Year: Unknown
Condition: Good

Longdon L. Miller Bridge has vertical-plank siding and a tin-covered gable roof. Its trussing has been supported by bracing in recent years.

Mays, Blaney Bridge

Location: On township route 423 southeast of West Alexander in Donegal Township.

Stream: Middle Wheeling Creek
Ownership: County
Truss type: Queenpost
Length: 31 ft. 6 in.

Width: 11 ft. 10 in.
Builder: Unknown
Year: Unknown
Condition: Good

Named for J. Blaney, who once owned land east of the bridge, the Blaney Bridge has vertical-plank siding and is a typical Washington County covered bridge.

Martin's Mill Bridge

Location: Was located west of Bissell in Amwell Township.

Stream: Ten Mile Creek
Ownership: County
Truss type: Queenpost
Length: 72 ft.

Width: 14 ft. 3 in.
Builder: Unknown
Year: 1888

Martin's Mill Bridge was the longest remaining covered bridge in the county. The bridge replaced an earlier covered bridge, which was destroyed by a flood in 1850. This bridge is no longer extant.

Plant's Bridge

Location: On township route 408 west of East Finley in East Finley Township.

Stream: Templeton Fork of Wheeling Creek
Ownership: County
Truss type: Kingpost
Length: 24 ft. 6 in.

Width: 12 ft. 10 in.
Builder: Unknown
Year: Unknown
Condition: Good

Plant's is a typical Washington County bridge which is in good condition.

Ralston Freeman Bridge

Location: On township route 352 northwest of Boyd in Hanover Township.

Stream: Aunt Clara's Fork of Kings Creek
Ownership: County
Truss type: Kingpost
Length: 28 ft.

Width: 12 ft.
Builder: Unknown
Year: 1915
Condition: Excellent

Because of a shortage of steel during World War I, Washington County continued to build covered wooden bridges. The Ralston Bridge is one of these bridges.

Mays, Blaney Bridge

Wilson's Mill Bridge

Location: On township route 486 east of West Middletown Station between Cross Creek and Hopewell townships.

Stream: Cross Creek
Ownership: County
Truss type: Kingpost
Length: 35 ft.

Width: 13 ft.
Builder: Unknown
Year: 1889
Condition: Good

This bridge has full vertical-plank siding and a tin-covered gable roof. It was moved to its present location in 1978 as part of a flood-control project.

Wyit Sprowls Bridge

Location: On township route 360 north of West Finley in West Finley Township.

Stream: Robinson Fork of Wheeling
  Creek
Ownership: County
Truss type: Queenpost
Length: 43 ft.

Width: 11 ft. 6 in.
Builder: Unknown
Year: Unknown
Condition: Good

Set in an attractive wooded valley, the Wyit Sprowls Bridge is of the typical Washington County design.

Wyit Sprowls Bridge

Wright, Cerl Bridge

Location: On township route 802 just south of Interstate 70, northeast of Vanceville in Somerset Township.

Stream: North Fork of Pigeon Creek
Ownership: County
Truss type: Kingpost
Length: 26 ft.

Width: 13 ft. 4 in.
Builder: Unknown
Year: Unknown
Condition: Good

This bridge has vertical-plank siding and a tin-covered gable roof. Its cut-stone abutments have been supported by concrete braces.

Sawhill Bridge

Location: On township route 426 southwest of Taylorstown in Blaine Township.

Stream: Buffalo Creek
Ownership: County
Truss type: Queenpost
Length: 49 ft.

Width: 12 ft. 6 in.
Builder: Unknown
Year: 1915
Condition: Good

Typical in design, the Sawhill Bridge was also built as a result of the shortage of steel during the war years.

Pine Bank Bridge

Location: In Meadowcroft Village, Avella, Jefferson Township.

Stream: crosses ravine
Ownership: Private
Truss type: Kingpost
Length: 30 ft. 6 in.

Width: 15 ft.
Builder: Unknown
Year: 1870
Condition: Good

This vertical-plank-sided, gable-roofed bridge was originally located over Toms Run in Gilmore Township and was moved to Meadowcroft Village by Albert Miller in 1962.

Bells Mills Bridge

Location: On S.R. 3061 at Bells Mills between Sewickley and South Huntingdon townships.

Stream: Sewickley Creek
Ownership: County
Truss type: Burr
Length: 95 ft.

Width: 14 ft.
Builder: Daniel McCain
Year: 1850
Condition: Good

This unusual bridge actually possesses an architectural style. Built in 1850 by architect and builder Daniel McCain, the Bells Mills Bridge was built in the Greek Revival style, with its plain pilaster and pedimented gable portals and horizontal clapboard siding. It also is the only remaining covered bridge in Westmoreland County.

Bells Mills Bridge

South Central

R·E·G·I·O·N

The South Central Region of Pennsylvania, drained by the Susquehanna River and Potomac River watersheds, has sixty-three covered bridges. The majority of the bridges in this region use the Burr-arch truss. The Susquehanna River watershed once had and still has the most covered bridges in the state.

Theodore Burr, the Connecticut-born designer of the truss which bears his name, tested his truss five times in colossal bridges spanning the Susquehanna River. His bridge at McCall's Ferry is thought to have been the longest single-span bridge in the world with a 360-foot, 4-inch clear span.

The Old Camelback Bridge, another of Burr's works, crossed the Susquehanna at Harrisburg. This undulating bridge, with its many Burr-arch trusses, was quite an experience to cross until its destruction in 1903. Unfortunately, none of the massive Susquehanna River bridges remains today. But this region offers many well-preserved Burr arch-, kingpost- and Town-truss bridges on a smaller scale. Lancaster and Perry counties have the most covered bridges in this region.

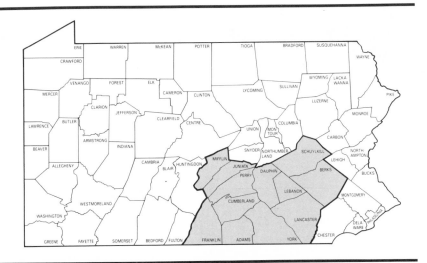

Sauck's (Sachs) Bridge

Location: On township route 326 (Water Works Road) southwest of Gettysburg, spanning Cumberland and Freedom townships.

Stream: Marsh Creek
Ownership: County
Truss type: Town
Length: 100 ft.

Width: 15 ft. 4 in.
Builder: Unknown
Year: c. 1854
Condition: Good

At the time of the Battle of Gettysburg this span was known as Saucks Bridge. On the night of July 3, 1863, General Robert E. Lee marched the major portion of his army over this bridge when he retreated from the battlefield after the defeat of Pickett's charge. The bridge was also used by Union troops during the Gettysburg Campaign. It was on the route used by Rowley's Division of the Union 1st Corps, the brigades of Biddle and Stone and Cooper's Battery.

Sauck's Bridge

Anderson's Farm Bridge

Location: On private land just off S.R. 1012 about 2 miles south of Bermudian in Latimore Township.

Stream: formerly over Mud Run, now on dry land
Ownership: Private
Truss type: Burr
Length: 79 ft.

Width: 14 ft.
Builder: Unknown
Year: Unknown
Condition: Good

Located not far from the Adams-York County line, this Burr-arch bridge is closed to traffic and is currently used as a storage shed.

Jack's Mountain Bridge

Location: On S.R. 3021 about 2 miles southwest of Fairfield in Hamiltonban Township.

Stream: Toms Creek
Ownership: State
Truss type: Burr
Length: 75 ft.

Width: 14 ft. 6 in.
Builder: Joseph Smith
Year: 1890
Condition: Excellent

Jack's Mountain Bridge has horizontal siding, cut-stone abutments and wide, longitudinally laid plank flooring. Its gable roof is tin covered and its Burr-arch trusses reach almost to eave level. This bridge was rehabilitated in 1992 to handle heavier traffic.

Conewago Chapel Bridge

Location: Was located about one mile southeast of Irishtown, spanning Mt. Pleasant and Conewago townships.

Stream: South Branch of Conewago Creek
Ownership: State
Truss type: Burr
Length: 98 ft.

Width: 13 ft. 3 in.
Builder: J. F. Socks
Year: 1899

This bridge was similar in style and construction to the Jack's Mountain Bridge, but with vertical rather than horizontal siding. It was destroyed by fire on June 14, 1985.

Kuhn's Fording Bridge

Location: On township route 552 one mile southwest of East Berlin, spanning Hamilton and Reading townships.

Stream: formerly over Conewago Creek
Ownership: County

Width: 16 ft.
Builder: Jas. Smith, William Leas
Year: 1897

Truss type: Burr
Length: 228 ft.

Condition: Ruins

Kuhn's Fording was the largest of the remaining covered bridges in Adams County until it was swept off its abutments on September 9, 1975 by flood, despite the efforts of concerned citizens to save it.

Heikes Bridge

Location: On township route 585 about 3 miles southwest of York Springs, spanning Tyrone and Huntingdon townships.

Stream: Bermudian Creek
Ownership: Private
Truss type: Burr
Length: 67 ft.

Width: 14 ft.
Builder: Unknown
Year: 1892
Condition: Fair

Located just off township route 585, the Heikes Bridge is no longer used for transportation purposes and is part of a private farm. This Burr arch-truss bridge has horizontal siding with an unusual mid-wall row of windows similar to the Sauck's Bridge.

Heikes Bridge

Pleasantville Bridge $P'S \ 2/28/98$

Location: On township route 360, Covered Bridge Road, in Pleasantville, Oley Township.

Stream: Little Manatawny Creek **Width:** 16 ft.
Ownership: State **Builder:** David Renno, Jonathan
Truss type: Burr   Bitner, Levi Marks
Length: 128 ft.   **Year:** 1852, 1856
            Condition: Good

This bridge was originally built in 1852 by David Renno as an open wooden bridge, one lane, one span, 128 ft. long. The bridge was not originally covered due to a lumber shortage during the 1850's, resulting from the Great Flood of 1850. By 1856, however, the bridge had been covered by Jonathan Bitner. This action necessitated the addition of a third arch and additional sets of supporting posts. Bitner's name as builder was seen over one portal, while Renno's was shown over the other portal. These tablets are now located in the abutments.

Pleasantville Bridge

Dreibelbis Station Bridge P's 2/28/98

Location: On township route 372, between Windsor and Balthaser roads, Greenwich Township.

Stream: Maiden Creek
Ownership: County
Truss type: Burr
Length: 172 ft.

Width: 16 ft.
Builder: Unknown
Year: 1869
Condition: Good

This is an unusual bridge, with stepped portals and horizontal siding.

Dreibelbis Station Bridge

Kutz's Mill Bridge P's 2/28/98

Location: On township route 798, Kutz Mill Road, northwest of Kutztown in Greenwich Township.

Stream: Sacony Creek
Ownership: County
Truss type: Burr
Length: 93 ft.

Width: 16 ft.
Builder: Bitner and Ahrens
Year: 1854
Condition: Good

The Kutz's Mill Bridge was built in 1854 and reinforced with a steel deck and beams in 1959. This bridge has a unique portal design, the only one of this style in Pennsylvania. It is also the oldest remaining covered bridge in Berks County.

Wertz's Bridge

Wertz's Bridge P'S 2/28/98

Location: On township route 362 northwest of Reading between Bern and Spring townships.

Stream: Tulpehocken Creek
Ownership: County
Truss type: Burr
Length: 165, 204 ft.

Width: 15 ft.
Builder: Amandas Knerr
Year: 1867
Condition: Fair

The Wertz's Bridge is also known as Red Covered Bridge and was built in 1867 by contractor Amandas Knerr at a price of $7,650. This bridge not only crosses Tulpehocken Creek but during the years 1867-1884 ran along the Union Canal. It is constructed with white-pine lumber and pinned with oak pins soaked in pine tar. Records show two lengths for this bridge.

Greisemer's Mill Bridge P'S 2/28/98

Location: On township route 634 east of Spangsville in Oley Township.

Stream: Manatawny Creek
Ownership: County
Truss type: Burr
Length: 124 ft.

Width: 14 ft. 6 in.
Builder: Unknown
Year: c. 1832
Condition: Excellent

This bridge is in excellent condition following repairs in 1957 and 1971.

Greisemer's Mill Bridge

CUMBERLAND COUNTY

Thompson Bridge

Location: Was located on township route 393 north of Green Spring between North Newtown and Upper Mifflin townships.

Stream: Conodoguinet Creek
Ownership: County
Truss type: Burr
Length: 149 ft. 6 in.

Width: 14 ft.
Builder: Unknown
Year: 1853

This bridge is no longer extant.

Ramp Bridge

Location: On township route 374 southeast of Newburg in Hopewell Township.

Stream: Conodoguinet Creek
Ownership: County

Width: 14 ft.
Builder: Unknown

| Truss type: Burr | Year: 1870 |
| Length: 130 ft. | Condition: Good |

This bridge has vertical-plank siding on the sidewalls and horizontal siding in the portals.

Bowmansdale Bridge

Location: On Messiah College campus, Grantham.

Stream: Yellow Breeches Creek	Width: 15 ft.
Ownership: Private	Builder: Unknown
Truss type: Burr	Year: 1867, 1971
Length: 112 ft.	Condition: Good

The Bowmansdale Bridge was moved to the Messiah College campus and rebuilt in 1971 by students. The timber deck has been replaced by a cement and steel deck. While this bridge cannot be considered historic due to its extensive rehabilitation, it is one of the last two covered bridges in Cumberland County.

Thompson Bridge

Everhart Bridge

Location: Museum grounds of the Fort Hunter Mansion, route 147, Fort Hunter.

Stream: on dry land
Ownership: County
Truss type: Kingpost
Length: 36 ft.

Width: 14 ft.
Builder: Unknown
Year: Unknown
Condition: Fair

This small kingpost-truss bridge was moved to the Fort Hunter Mansion grounds in 1940. It has now been dismantled and is in storage.

Everhart Bridge

Henninger Farm Bridge

Location: On township route 624 northeast of Elizabethville in Washington Township.

Stream: Wiconisco Creek
Ownership: County
Truss type: Burr
Length: 72 ft.

Width: 16 ft.
Builder: Unknown
Year: Unknown
Condition: Good

The Henninger Farm Bridge is the only remaining covered bridge in Dauphin County in its original location. This Burr-arch bridge has vertical-plank siding and a gable roof. It spans Wiconisco Creek in the upper part of the county. The Wiconisco Creek was crossed by nine covered bridges as late as 1971; however, the flood caused by Hurricane Agnes in 1972 destroyed all but this bridge.

Henninger Farm Bridge

Martin's Mill Bridge

Location: On township route 341 southwest of Greencastle in Antrim Township.

Stream: Conococheague Creek
Ownership: Private
Truss type: Town
Length: 200 ft, 2 spans

Width: 16 ft.
Builder: Jacob Shirk
Year: 1839
Condition: Good

The Martin's Mill Bridge is the longest Town-truss covered bridge remaining in Pennsylvania. This two-span bridge has horizontal siding and square stepped portals. The bridge was heavily damaged in the Agnes Flood of 1972 and has been completely reassembled and restored.

Martin's Mill Bridge (during reconstruction)

Witherspoon Red Bridge

Location: On township route 328 southeast of Mercersburg in Montgomery Township.

Stream: Licking Creek
Ownership: County
Truss type: Burr
Length: 73 ft.

Width: 14 ft.
Builder: S. Stouffer
Year: 1883
Condition: Good

The Witherspoon Bridge has vertical-plank siding and a gable roof. Northeast of this bridge is a fine stone-arch bridge known as Hays Bridge.

JUNIATA COUNTY

(See also Juniata/Snyder Counties)

Academia, Pomeroy Bridge

Location: On township route 349 south of Academia between Beale and Spruce Hill townships.

Stream: Tuscarora Creek
Ownership: Private
Truss type: Burr
Length: 270 ft, 2 spans

Width: 15 ft. 6 in.
Builder: James M. Groninger
Year: 1902
Condition: Excellent

This large, two-span covered bridge has vertical siding and open windows at the eave level. Academia is one of the longest of the remaining covered bridges in Pennsylvania. Its length is often recorded as 305 feet.

Dimmsville Bridge

Location: On S.R. 2017 northeast of Dimmsville in Greenwood Township.

Stream: Cocolamus Creek
Ownership: Private
Truss type: Burr
Length: 90 ft.

Width: 15 ft.
Builder: Unknown
Year: 1902
Condition: Excellent

The Dimmsville Bridge has vertical siding, eave-level windows and square windows in the center of each sidewall.

Lehman's, Port Royal Bridge

Location: On township route 451 west of Port Royal in Milford Township.

Stream: Licking Creek
Ownership: Private
Truss type: Stringer (Burr ornamental)
Length: 100 ft, 2 spans

Width: 15 ft. 6 in.
Builder: Unknown
Year: 1888
Condition: Good

The Lehman's, Port Royal Bridge is a two-span bridge using two Burr-arch trusses placed end to end. This bridge was badly damaged during the Agnes Flood of 1972 and was rebuilt using original timbers.

Lehman's, Port Royal Bridge

Mercer's Mill Bridge

Location: On township route 976 south of Christiana between West Fallowfield Township, Chester County, and Sadsbury Township, Lancaster County.

Stream: Octoraro Creek
Ownership: Two counties
Truss type: Burr
Length: 86 ft.

Width: 15 ft.
Builder: B. J. Carter
Year: 1880
Condition: Good

The Mercer's Mill Bridge has vertical-plank siding, and horizontal siding in the portals.

Pine Grove Bridge

Location: On S.R. 2006 at Pine Grove, between East Nottingham Township, Chester County, and Little Britain Township, Lancaster County.

Stream: Octoraro Creek
Ownership: State
Truss type: Burr
Length: 178 ft., 2 spans

Width: 15 ft.
Builder: Elias McMellen
Year: 1884
Condition: Fair

One of the longest covered bridges in the state, the Pine Grove Bridge is perhaps the only one left in the state similar to the famous camel-back bridges. The two Burr-arch spans do bow slightly, giving riders a feeling of what some of our more famous bridges were like, one of which was the Camelback Bridge that crossed the Susquehanna River at Harrisburg.

LANCASTER COUNTY

(See also Lancaster/Chester Counties)

Pool Forge Bridge

Location: On township route 773 north of Beartown in Caernarvon Township.

Stream: Conestoga River
Ownership: Private
Truss type: Burr
Length: 84 ft.

Width: 15 ft.
Builder: Levi Fink
Year: 1859
Condition: Fair

The Pool Forge Bridge is located just off township route 773 and carries only foot traffic as the bridge has been by-passed. Its vertical-plank siding is open at the top leaving an open window area under the eaves.

Pool Forge Bridge

Weaver's Mill Bridge

Location: On township route 773 north of Goodville in Caernarvon Township.

Stream: Conestoga River
Ownership: County
Truss type: Burr
Length: 79 ft.

Width: 15 ft.
Builder: B. C. Carter
Year: 1878
Condition: Fair

Crossing the Conestoga River, the Weaver's Mill Bridge sits on cut-stone abutments. Its vertical, board-and-batten siding and shingle-covered gable roof both need repairs. Its simple triangular-shaped portals have vertical board-and-batten siding.

Kurtz's Mill Bridge

Location: In Williamson Park south of the city of Lancaster in West Lampeter Township.

Stream: Mill Creek
Ownership: County
Truss type: Burr
Length: 90 ft.

Width: 15 ft.
Builder: W. W. Upp
Year: 1876
Condition: Good

Following the Agnes Flood of 1972, this bridge was moved by trailer fifteen miles from its original site to Williamson Park. The moving cost was $5,000 and its restoration cost was $55,000. It was rededicated on April 22, 1975.

Bitzer's Mill, Eberly's Mill Bridge

Location: On S.R. 1013 north of Fairmount in West Earl Township.

Stream: Conestoga River
Ownership: State
Truss type: Burr
Length: 87 ft.

Width: 15 ft.
Builder: George Fink, Samuel
Reamsnyder
Year: 1846
Condition: Good

Bitzer's Mill Bridge is identical in styling to the Weaver's Mill Bridge, with its vertical board-and-batten siding and triangular portals, but is in much better condition.

Pinetown, Bushong's Mill Bridge

Location: On township route 620 southeast of Oregon between Upper Leacock and Manheim townships.

Stream: Conestoga River
Ownership: County
Truss type: Burr
Length: 120 ft.

Width: 15 ft.
Builder: Elias McMellen
Year: 1867
Condition: Good

Washed off its abutments in the Agnes Flood of 1972, it was replaced and rebuilt at a cost of $40,000. It was necessary to raise the bridge several feet, but other than that it retains its original style and integrity.

Erb's Bridge

Location: On township route 634 west of Akron between Clay and Warwick townships.

Stream: Hammer Creek
Ownership: County
Truss type: Burr
Length: 70 ft.

Width: 15 ft.
Builder: John G. Bowman
Year: 1887
Condition: Good

Erb's Bridge has vertical board-and-batten siding, cut-stone abutments and window openings under the eaves.

Red Run Mill, Oberhaltzer's Bridge

Location: West of township route 816, south of Red Run in Earl Township.

Stream: Muddy Creek
Ownership: Private
Truss type: Burr
Length: 104 ft.

Width: 15 ft.
Builder: Elias McMellen
Year: 1866
Condition: Poor

The Red Run Mill Bridge has been by-passed and is closed to all traffic. This vertical-plank-sided bridge is in very poor condition.

Erb's Bridge

Bucher's Mill Bridge

Location: On township route 955 southwest of Reamstown in East Cocalico Township.

Stream: Cocalico Creek
Ownership: County
Truss type: Burr
Length: 64 ft.

Width: 15 ft.
Builder: Elias McMellen
Year: 1881, 1892
Condition: Excellent

Located in a broad valley, the Bucher's Mill Bridge has vertical board-and-batten siding. This picturesque bridge is in excellent condition.

Guy Bard's, Keller's Bridge

Location: On township route 656 northwest of Akron in Ephrata Township.

Stream: Cocalico Creek
Ownership: County
Truss type: Burr
Length: 63 ft.

Width: 15 ft.
Builder: Elias McMellen
Year: 1891
Condition: Excellent

In excellent condition, the Keller Bridge has vertical board-and-batten siding and horizontal siding in its portals. Locally known as Guy Bard's bridge, the bridge was named for a leading Pennsylvania jurist who once lived nearby.

Zook's Mill Bridge

Zook's Mill Bridge

Location: On township route 797 northeast of Oregon between Warwick and Ephrata townships.

Stream: Cocalico Creek
Ownership: County
Truss type: Burr
Length: 75 ft.

Width: 15 ft.
Builder: Henry Zook
Year: 1849
Condition: Good

One of Lancaster County's early covered bridges, the Zook's Mill Bridge has been well maintained over the years. The bridge has very high, vertical-plank sidewalls leaving only a narrow window opening under the eaves.

Buck Hill Bridge

Location: Off township route 501 on private land, south of Kissel Hill in Warwick Township.

Stream: Pond
Ownership: Private
Truss type: Burr
Length: 47 ft.

Width: 15 ft.
Builder: Theodore D. Cochran
Year: 1844
Condition: Good

Located on private farmland, the Buck Hill Bridge is closed to all traffic, but can be seen from route 501 in the winter or early spring when the trees are bare.

Landis Mill Bridge

Location: On township route 560 west of Oreville between East Hempfield Township and the city of Lancaster.

Stream: Little Conestoga Creek
Ownership: County
Truss type: Kingpost
Length: 40 ft.

Width: 15 ft.
Builder: Elias McMellen
Year: 1878
Condition: Good

The Landis Mill Bridge is a fine example of a multiple kingpost-truss bridge, rare in Lancaster County. Today this bridge is completely surrounded by modern development and has lost much of its rural charm and setting.

White Rock Bridge

Location: On township route 337 east of White Rock between Little Britain and Colerain townships.

Stream: West Branch of Octoraro
Creek
Ownership: County
Truss type: Burr
Length: 103 ft.

Width: 15 ft.
Builder: Elias McMellen
Year: 1847
Condition: Good

The White Rock Bridge is perhaps the most attractive of the remaining covered bridges in Lancaster County. This is mainly due to its beautiful rural setting.

Leaman Place, Eshelman's Mill Bridge

Location: On township route 684 northeast of Paradise between Paradise and Leacock townships.

Stream: Pequea Creek	**Width:** 15 ft.
Ownership: County	**Builder:** Elias McMellen
Truss type: Burr	**Year:** 1893
Length: 103 ft.	**Condition:** Excellent

Located in the open farmland of southeastern Lancaster County, the Leaman Place Bridge is a popular stopping place for tourists to the "Pennsylvania Dutch" area of Lancaster County. The bridge has the typical vertical-plank siding, but has board-and-batten siding in the portal ends.

Herr's Mill, Soudersburg Bridge

Herr's Mill, Soudersburg Bridge

Location: On township route 696 southwest of Soudersburg between Paradise and Leacock townships.

Stream: Pequea Creek
Ownership: Private
Truss type: Burr
Length: 166 ft., 2 spans

Width: 15 ft.
Builder: Joseph Elliot, Robert Russell
Year: 1885
Condition: Excellent

The Soudersburg Bridge has two Burr-arch spans, vertical siding and cut-stone abutments. The bridge has been by-passed by township route 696. It has an unusual side entrance from an adjoining road and several side windows with awnings.

Neff's Mill Bridge

Location: On township route 559 north of Lime Valley between West Lampeter and Strasburg townships.

Stream: Pequea Creek
Ownership: County
Truss type: Burr
Length: 91 ft.

Width: 15 ft.
Builder: James C. Carpenter
Year: 1875
Condition: Excellent

The Neff's Mill Bridge is in excellent condition with vertical-plank siding and fine, cut-stone abutments.

Lime Valley Bridge

Location: On township route 498 in Lime Valley between West Lampeter and Strasburg townships.

Stream: Pequea Creek
Ownership: County
Truss type: Burr
Length: 91 ft.

Width: 15 ft.
Builder: Elias McMellen
Year: 1871
Condition: Good

This attractive Burr-arch bridge is located in the small community of Lime Valley. Many of Pennsylvania's covered bridges, especially those in Lancaster County, are or were associated with mills. The Lime Valley mill is in excellent condition and is a fine example of a stone gristmill.

Baumgardner's Mill Bridge

Location: On township route 425 east of Marticville between Pequea and Martic township.

Stream: Pequea Creek
Ownership: County

Width: 15 ft.
Builder: Unknown

Truss type: Burr
Length: 94 ft.

Year: 1860, 1987
Condition: Good

The Burr-arch Baumgardner's Bridge is in good condition; however, the mill for which it was named is in ruins on the bank near the bridge. This bridge was rehabilitated in 1987 by Lancaster County.

Colemanville Bridge

Location: On township route 408 south of Colemanville between Conestoga and Martic townships.

Stream: Pequea Creek
Ownership: County
Truss type: Burr
Length: 155 ft.

Width: 15 ft.
Builder: Unknown
Year: 1856
Condition: Excellent

This attractive bridge is located in a wooded valley near the entrance to Susquehannock State Park. One of the longest covered bridges in Lancaster County, this bridge was washed off its abutments during the Agnes Flood of 1972. Lifted with the help of two cranes and repaired by Amish carpenters, the bridge was rededicated on December 10, 1973.

Forry's Mill Bridge

Location: On township route 362 northwest of Ironville between Rapho and West Hempfield townships.

Stream: Chickies Creek
Ownership: County
Truss type: Burr
Length: 90 ft.

Width: 15 ft.
Builder: Elias McMellen
Year: 1869
Condition: Fair

The Forry's Mill Bridge has the typical vertical board-and-batten siding and cut-stone abutments.

Schenck's Mill Bridge

Location: On township route 372 northwest of Landisville between Rapho and East Hempfield townships.

Stream: Chickies Creek
Ownership: County
Truss type: Burr
Length: 80 ft.

Width: 15 ft.
Builder: Levi Fink
Year: 1855
Condition: Excellent

The Schenck's Mill Bridge is unusual in Lancaster County, with its horizontal-clapboard siding. It also has four rectangular windows with wooden awnings on its east-bank end. The mill and miller's house, with which the bridge is associated, are in excellent condition and help to create a nineteenth-century atmosphere for the bridge.

Schenck's Mill Bridge

Shearer's Bridge

Location: In High School Memorial Park, Manheim, between Penn and Rapho townships.

Stream: Chickies Creek
Ownership: County
Truss type: Burr
Length: 73 ft.

Width: 15 ft.
Builder: Jacob Clare
Year: 1856, 1971
Condition: Excellent

Closed to all but foot traffic, the Shearer's Bridge is in excellent condition. It was moved to its present location in 1971.

Kaufman's Distillery Bridge

Location: On township route 889 northeast of Sporting Hill between Rapho and Penn townships.

Stream: Chickies Creek
Ownership: County
Truss type: Burr
Length: 84 ft.

Width: 15 ft.
Builder: Elias McMellen
Year: 1874
Condition: Good

Once associated with a local distillery, the bridge today is located in open farmland near the small community of Sporting Hill.

Jackson's Mill Bridge

Location: On township route 696 west of Bartville in Bart Township.

Stream: West Octoraro Creek
Ownership: County
Truss type: Burr
Length: 156 ft.

Width: 15 ft.
Builder: John Smith, Samuel Stauffer
Year: 1878, 1984
Condition: Excellent

One of the most attractive covered bridges, the Jackson's Mill Bridge is located in the heart of the Amish country of southeastern Lancaster County. Located just west of the small community of Bartville, with its Amish school, the bridge is one of Lancaster's longer Burr arch-truss bridges. It was damaged by flood July 1, 1984, and was rebuilt by the township.

Hunsecker's Mill Bridge

Location: On S.R. 1029, Hunsecker, between Manheim and Upper Leacock townships.

Stream: Conestoga River
Ownership: State
Truss type: Burr
Length: 172 ft.

Width: 15 ft.
Builder: Joseph Russell
Year: 1843, 1973
Condition: Excellent

Destroyed in Agnes Flood of 1972, this bridge was completely rebuilt by the Pennsylvania Department of Transportation in 1973.

Risser's Mill Bridge

Location: On S.R. 4010, between Mount Joy and Rapho townships.

Stream: Chickies Creek
Ownership: State
Truss type: Burr
Length: 70 ft.

Width: 15 ft.
Builder: Elias McMellen
Year: 1849
Condition: Good

This bridge has vertical-plank siding and gable roof.

Seigrist's Mill Bridge

Location: On township route 360 north of Ironville between Rapho and West Hempfield townships.

Stream: Chickies Creek
Ownership: County
Truss type: Burr
Length: 91 ft.

Width: 15 ft.
Builder: James C. Carpenter
Year: 1885
Condition: Good

Seigrist Mill Bridge has vertical board-and-batten siding and portal ends, cut-stone abutments and a gable roof.

Willow Hill Bridge

Location: Just off U.S. 30 east of Lancaster in East Lampeter Township.

Stream: branch of Mill Creek
Ownership: Private
Truss type: Burr
Length: 64 ft.

Width: 15 ft.
Builder: Roy Zimmerman
Year: 1962
Condition: Excellent

This bridge was reconstructed using parts from two separate covered bridges. It has board-and-batten siding and stone abutments.

PERRY COUNTY

Bistline, Flickinger's Mill Bridge

Location: On S.R. 3005 south of Andersonburg in Southwest Madison Township.

Stream: Shermans Creek
Ownership: State
Truss type: Burr
Length: 96 ft.

Width: 13 ft. 6 in.
Builder: Unknown
Year: 1871
Condition: Good

This Burr-arch bridge has rough vertical-plank siding on its sidewalls and portals. In recent years it has been reinforced with steel beams.

Adairs, Cisna Mill Bridge

Location: On S.R. 3008 south of Cisna Run in Southwest Madison Township.

Stream: Shermans Creek
Ownership: State
Truss type: Burr
Length: 150 ft.

Width: 14 ft. 3 in.
Builder: Unknown
Year: 1864, rebuilt 1919
Condition: Good

The second-longest bridge in the county, the Adairs Bridge also has rough, vertical siding. This bridge has been reinforced with steel beams.

Red Bridge

Location: On S.R. 1005 west of Liverpool in Liverpool Township.

Stream: Wild Cat Creek
Ownership: Private
Truss type: Kingpost
Length: 55 ft.

Width: 15 ft.
Builder: Unknown
Year: 1886
Condition: Good

The Red Bridge has been by-passed by its highway and now sits on the side of the road in fairly good condition. It has vertical-plank siding and a wooden-shingle-covered gable roof.

Adairs, Cisna Mill Bridge

Saville Bridge

Location: On S.R. 4001 south of Saville in Saville Township.

Stream: Big Buffalo Creek
Ownership: State
Truss type: Burr
Length: 60 ft.

Width: 17 ft.
Builder: L. M. Wentzel
Year: 1903
Condition: Fair

The Saville Bridge is one of Perry County's newer covered bridges. Similar to Adairs Bridge in styling, it is in need of repair.

Kochendefer Bridge

Location: On township route 332 south of Saville in Saville Township.

Stream: Big Buffalo Creek
Ownership: County
Truss type: Kingpost, Queenpost
Length: 72 ft.

Width: 18 ft.
Builder: Adair Brothers
Year: 1919
Condition: Excellent

Built at a cost of $2,380 in 1919, the Kochendefer Bridge is located on the same road as the Saville Bridge. This wide bridge has very narrow portals, adding to its broad appearance.

Rice, Landisburg Bridge

Location: On township route 333 southeast of Landisburg in Tyrone Township.

Stream: Shermans Creek
Ownership: County
Truss type: Burr, Queenpost
Length: 124 ft.

Width: 18 ft.
Builder: Unknown
Year: 1869
Condition: Excellent

This unusual bridge combines the use of queenpost trusses and Burr-arch trusses in an unusual way. Beneath the large Burr arches are located two smaller queenpost trusses.

New Germantown Bridge

Location: On township route 302 south of New Germantown in Jackson Township.

Stream: Shermans Creek
Ownership: County
Truss type: Kingpost, Queenpost
Length: 74 ft.

Width: 12 ft.
Builder: John W. Fry
Year: 1891
Condition: Excellent

This attractive bridge has vertical-plank siding and a tin-covered gable roof. The portals have been painted in stripes, adding to its rather special appearance.

New Germantown Bridge

Mt. Pleasant Bridge

Location: On township route 304 south of Mt. Pleasant in Jackson Township.

Stream: Shermans Creek
Ownership: County
Truss type: Kingpost, Queenpost
Length: 60 ft.

Width: 17 ft. 9 in.
Builder: L. M. Wentzel
Year: 1918
Condition: Good

The Mt. Pleasant Bridge has vertical-plank siding with window openings under the eaves. It has been reinforced with steel beams in recent years.

Book's, Kaufman Bridge

Location: On S.R. 3003 between Mt. Pleasant and Blain in Jackson Township.

Stream: Shermans Creek
Ownership: State
Truss type: Burr
Length: 70 ft.

Width: 17 ft.
Builder: Unknown
Year: 1884
Condition: Good

Similar to other Perry County covered bridges, the Book's Bridge also has rough, vertical-plank siding.

Mt. Pleasant Bridge

Book's, Kaufman Bridge

Enslow, Turkey Tail Bridge

Location: On township route 312 south of Blain in Jackson Township.

Stream: Shermans Creek
Ownership: County
Truss type: Burr
Length: 110 ft.

Width: 16 ft. 11 in.
Builder: Unknown
Year: 1904
Condition: Good

Built in 1904 at a cost of $2,250, this bridge has been reinforced with twenty-four-inch steel beams.

Waggoner Mill Bridge

Location: On township route 579 east of Fort Robinson between Tyrone and Northeast Madison townships.

Stream: Bixlers Run
Ownership: Private
Truss type: Burr
Length: 77 ft.

Width: 17 ft.
Builder: Joseph D. Lightner
Year: 1889
Condition: Good

This setting is what makes the Waggoner Mill Bridge so attractive. This Burr-arch bridge is located near the remains of the Waggoner Mill, a large, well-preserved stone gristmill. The dam and race are still present and contribute to the attractiveness of the setting.

Waggoner Mill Bridge

Dellville Bridge

Location: On township route 456 south of Dellville, in Wheatfield Township.

Stream: Shermans Creek
Ownership: County
Truss type: Burr
Length: 174 ft.

Width: 20 ft.
Builder: Andrew Clouser
Year: 1889
Condition: Excellent

Dellville Bridge is the largest in the county, both in length and width. Set high above the stream, the bridge has large stone abutments and vertical-plank siding.

Fleisher Bridge

Location: On township route 477 northwest of Milford in Oliver Township.

>**Stream:** Big Buffalo Creek
>**Ownership:** County
>**Truss type:** Burr
>**Length:** 115 ft.

>**Width:** 17 ft.
>**Builder:** Yohn and Ritter
>**Year:** 1887
>**Condition:** Fair

One of the longest bridges in Perry County, this bridge is similar to other Perry County bridges in its design.

Clays, Wahneta Bridge

Location: On S.R. 1011 in Little Buffalo State Park, Centre Township.

>**Stream:** Little Buffalo Creek
>**Ownership:** State
>**Truss type:** Burr
>**Length:** 82 ft.

>**Width:** 15 ft.
>**Builder:** George Harting
>**Year:** 1890
>**Condition:** Good

The Clays Bridge is today located in Little Buffalo State Park.

SCHUYLKILL COUNTY

Zimmerman's Bridge

Location: On township route 526 west of Rock in Washington Township.

>**Stream:** Little Swatara Creek
>**Ownership:** County
>**Truss type:** Burr
>**Length:** 50 ft. 6 in.

>**Width:** 11 ft.
>**Builder:** Unknown
>**Year:** c. 1880
>**Condition:** Good

This bridge is one of the two remaining covered bridges in Schuylkill County. At one time there were fifty-one of these wooden spans in the county. It is identical to the Rock Bridge in styling.

Rock Bridge

Location: On township route 542 east of Rock in Washington Township.

>**Stream:** Little Swatara Creek
>**Ownership:** County
>**Truss type:** Burr
>**Length:** 39 ft.

>**Width:** 13 ft. 5 in.
>**Builder:** Unknown
>**Year:** 1870
>**Condition:** Good

This small Burr arch-truss bridge has vertical siding and a gable roof. Steel inside barriers have been added to protect the trussing system from traffic.

Zimmerman's Bridge

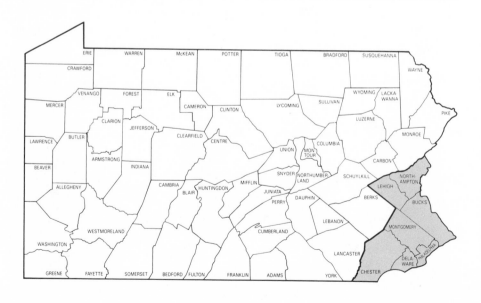

Southeast
R·E·G·I·O·N

Drained by the Delaware River watershed, the southeast region of Pennsylvania has thirty-two covered bridges. Some of Pennsylvania's most interesting portal designs remain in this region, offering not only a transportation and engineering interest to the study of covered bridges but an artistic interest as well.

Bucks County has the largest number of Town-truss bridges in the state. Whether it was the plan of the county commissioners or the preference of the local builders is not known. It is unusual to think of a covered bridge in a large city, but Philadelphia has one in Fairmount Park.

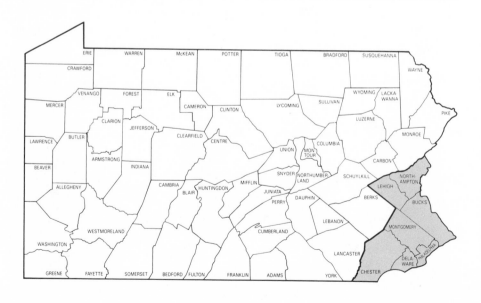

Haupt's Mill Bridge

Location: Was located in Durham, Durham Township.

Stream: Durham Creek
Ownership: County
Truss type: Town
Length: 107 ft.

Width: 15 ft.
Builder: Unknown
Year: 1872

In 1736, Henry Haupt, a miller from Germany, built his stone gristmill on the banks of Durham Creek. To service his mill a road and bridge were needed. Built utilizing the Town-truss system, this bridge reflected the type most common in Bucks county. It was destroyed by arson, January 1985.

Knecht's Bridge

Location: On township route 418 west of Durham in Springfield Township.

Stream: Durham Creek
Ownership: County
Truss type: Town
Length: 110 ft.

Width: 15 ft.
Builder: Unknown
Year: 1873
Condition: Good

Built of hemlock and on the route of the Walking Purchase, the Knecht's Bridge is identical in styling to what was the Haupt's Mill Bridge.

Haupt's Mill Bridge

Van Sant Bridge

Location: On township route 392 west of Washington Crossing State Park in Solebury Township.

Stream: Pidcock Creek	**Width:** 15 ft.
Ownership: County	**Builder:** G. Arnst & P. S. Naylor
Truss type: Town	**Year:** 1875
Length: 86 ft.	**Condition:** Good

Van Sant Bridge is located near Bowman's Hill and was often called Beaver Dam bridge. It is one of two which once crossed Pidcock Creek; the Neely Mill Bridge was removed in 1937. It is a typical Bucks County bridge with its Town truss, cut-stone abutments, gable roof, triangular or curved inner portal openings, inner wall siding in the portal area, and full exterior walls.

Erwinna Bridge

Location: On S.R. 1012 in Erwinna, Tinicum Township.

Stream: Lodi Creek	**Width:** 15 ft.
Ownership: State	**Builder:** Unknown
Truss type: Town	**Year:** 1871
Length: 56 ft.	**Condition:** Good

Built in 1871, the Erwinna Bridge is the shortest of the remaining covered bridges in the county, and is a fine example of the typical Bucks County-style covered bridge.

South Perkasie Bridge

Location: In Lenape Park in South Perkasie, Perkasie.

Stream: once over Pleasant Spring Creek, now over dry land	**Width:** 15 ft.
Ownership: Private	**Builder:** Unknown
Truss type: Town	**Year:** 1832
Length: 79 ft.	**Condition:** Good

The South Perkasie Bridge is the oldest covered bridge in the county. It once spanned Pleasant Spring Creek, but after being condemned for traffic it was removed to its present location through the efforts of the local historical society. It has an interesting warning sign: "$5.00 fine for any person riding or driving over this bridge faster than a walk or smoking a segar on."

Van Sant Bridge

Erwinna Bridge

South Perkasie Bridge

Sheard's Mill Bridge

Location: On S.R. 4099 in Thatcher between Haycock and East Rockhill townships.

Stream: Tohickon Creek
Ownership: State
Truss type: Town
Length: 113 ft.

Width: 15 ft.
Builder: Unknown
Year: 1873
Condition: Poor

Sheard's Mill Bridge is located at Thatcher and crosses Tohickon Creek. This typical Bucks County bridge is unfortunately in poor condition.

Mood's Bridge

Location: On S.R. 4089 east of Perkasie in East Rockhill Township.

Stream: northeast branch,
  Perkiomen Creek
Ownership: State
Truss type: Town
Length: 120 ft.

Width: 15 ft.
Builder: Unknown
Year: 1874
Condition: Good

Mood's Bridge is a fine example of a typical Bucks County covered bridge, but with wide vertical-plank siding and portals. This bridge was repaired in 1962.

Uhlerstown Bridge

Location: On township route 443, Uhlerstown, Tinicum Township.

Stream: Tinicum Creek
Ownership: County
Truss type: Town
Length: 102 ft.

Width: 15 ft.
Builder: Unknown
Year: 1832
Condition: Good

Built of oak, the Uhlerstown covered bridge is the only bridge in the county with side windows. Uhlerstown was once known as Mexico, but was later named for Michael Uhler, who owned a canal boat building yard and operated a string of canal boats. This bridge crosses the Delaware Canal.

Frankenfield Bridge

Location: On township route 440 south of Sundale in Tinicum Township.

Stream: Tinicum Creek
Ownership: County
Truss type: Town
Length: 130 ft.

Width: 12 ft.
Builder: David Sutton
Year: 1872
Condition: Excellent

The Frankenfield Bridge has been recently restored by the county. It has vertical-plank siding, gable roof, inside walls in the portal area and cut-stone abutments.

Cabin Run Bridge

Location: On township route 416 west of Ralph Stover State Park in Plumstead Township.

Stream: Cabin Run Creek
Ownership: County
Truss type: Town
Length: 82 ft.

Width: 15 ft.
Builder: David Sutton
Year: 1871
Condition: Fair

This Town-truss bridge is in fair condition and is typical of Bucks County bridges. Bucks County has the largest number of Town-truss bridges in Pennsylvania, eleven of Pennsylvania's seventeen.

Loux Bridge

Location: On S.R. 1003 southeast of Pipersville in Plumstead Township.

Stream: Cabin Run Creek
Ownership: State
Truss type: Town
Length: 71 ft.

Width: 15 ft.
Builder: David Sutton
Year: 1874
Condition: Fair

Loux Bridge

The second-shortest covered bridge in the county, the Loux Bridge has several distinctive features that distinguish it from the typical Bucks County covered bridge. Instead of a triangular portal opening, the Loux Bridge has an oval-shaped portal. The inside portal walls are also absent, as are the triangular abutment caps.

Pine Valley Bridge

Location: On township route 340 between the borough of New Britain and New Britain Township.

Stream: Pine Run Creek
Ownership: County
Truss type: Town
Length: 81 ft.

Width: 15 ft.
Builder: David Sutton
Year: 1842
Condition: Good

One of the earliest remaining covered bridges in the county, it is similar in style to other Bucks County bridges, and it cost $5,553 to build.

Twining Ford Bridge

Location: Was located in Tyler State Park between Northampton and Newtown townships.

Stream: Nechaminy Creek
Ownership: State
Truss type: Town
Length: 150 ft., 2 spans

Width: 17 ft.
Builder: Unknown
Year: Unknown

Built of hemlock, the Twining Ford Bridge was located within Tyler State Park. This was the longest remaining covered bridge in the county and was destroyed by fire on October 8, 1991.

Bartram's Bridge

CHESTER/DELAWARE COUNTIES

Bartram's Bridge

Location: On Goshen Road east of Echo Valley in Willistown Township, Chester County, and Newtown Township, Delaware County.

Stream: Crum Creek
Ownership: Private
Truss type: Burr
Length: 60 ft.

Width: 13 ft.
Builder: Ferdinand Wood
Year: 1860
Condition: Good

The Bartram's Bridge has unique slanted-plank portals, the only bridge in Pennsylvania with this unusual design. This bridge is also the only bridge remaining in Delaware County, a county which had thirty covered bridges. The bridge was closed to traffic in 1941 and preserved and restored by a local historical society and concerned citizens.

CHESTER COUNTY

(See also Lancaster/Chester Counties)
(See also Chester/Delaware Counties)

Rudolph and Arthur Bridge

Location: On township route 307 just north of the Pennsylvania-Maryland state line in New London and Elk townships.

Stream: Big Elk Creek
Ownership: County
Truss type: Burr
Length: 80 ft.

Width: 15 ft.
Builder: Menander Wood, Richard T. Meredith
Year: 1880
Condition: Good

Built in 1880, the Rudolph and Arthur Bridge has vertical-plank siding with eave-level window openings. This bridge was named for the paper firm of the families of Rudolph and Arthur, which was located just above the bridge on the east bank of the creek. The woodwork for the bridge was built by Menander Wood for $1,400, and the stonework was completed by Richard T. Meredith for the sum of $890.

Glen Hope Bridge

Location: On township route 344 west of Peacedale in Elk Township.

Stream: Little Elk Creek
Ownership: County
Truss type: Burr
Length: 65 ft.

Width: 16 ft.
Builder: Menander Wood, George E. Jones
Year: 1889, 1987
Condition: Good

The Glen Hope Bridge was built at a total cost of $1,767. This bridge is located only one-half mile from the Pennsylvania and Maryland state boundary and is located at Anderson's Ford, named for a local farmer, John Anderson. This bridge was damaged by fire on December 2, 1987 and has been rehabilitated.

Linton Stevens Bridge

Location: On township route 344 northeast of Hickory Hill in Nottingham and New London townships.

Stream: Big Elk Creek
Ownership: County
Truss type: Burr
Length: 102 ft.

Width: 15 ft.
Builder: Denithorne & Son
Year: 1886
Condition: Good

Named after the postmaster of Hickory Hill, the Linton Stevens Bridge has an unusual history. Originally a foot bridge crossed Big Elk Creek at this site. Later, in 1875, an iron bridge was built here by the county. However, that bridge was severely damaged by the 1884 flood and was replaced by the covered bridge which stands today.

Speakman No. 1 Bridge

Location: On S.R. 3047 south of Ercildoun in East Fallowfield Township.

Stream: Ruck Run
Ownership: State
Truss type: Burr
Length: 75 ft.

Width: 14 ft.
Builder: Menander Wood, Ferdinand Wood
Year: 1881
Condition: Good

This Burr-arch bridge is located in a remote valley, but once served the Jonathan Speakman gristmill, a mill converted from a paper mill to a gristmill in 1870. Built at a total cost of $2,000 the bridge is located only one and a half miles from the Speakman No. 2 Bridge.

Speakman No. 2, Mary Ann Pyle Bridge

Speakman No. 2, Mary Ann Pyle Bridge

Location: Off township route 371 on private land in East Fallowfield Township.

Stream: Buck Run
Ownership: Private
Truss type: Queenpost
Length: 75 ft.

Width: 15 ft.
Builder: Menander Wood,
    Ferdinand Wood
Year: 1881
Condition: Good

This and the Hayes Clark Bridge, located only one-fourth mile away, were called the "twin bridges." This bridge was named for the daughter of James B. Pyle, a local landowner. Its cost was $1,183 for woodwork and $755 for stonework. Located on private land, this bridge and the Hayes Clark Bridge are closed to traffic.

Hayes Clark Bridge

Location: Off township route 371 on private land east of Doe Run in East Fallowfield Township.

Stream: Doe Run
Ownership: Private
Truss type: Queenpost
Length: 75 ft.

Width: 16 ft.
Builder: Buck & Doe Run Valley
    Farms
Year: 1971
Condition: Excellent

76

The present Hayes Clark Bridge was constructed in 1971 following the burning of a covered bridge which stood on the site from 1884 to 1963. The 1884 bridge was a Burr-arch built by Menander Wood and Denithorne & Pollitt of Phoenixville for a total cost of $2,526. Two earlier bridges upstream bore the name Hayes Clark, but both were destroyed by floods. Hayes Clark once operated a 208-acre farm in the area.

Gibson's Bridge

Location: On township route 391 southwest of Harmony Hill in East Bradford and West Bradford townships.

Stream: East Branch, Brandywine Creek
Ownership: County
Truss type: Burr
Length: 78 ft.

Width: 14 ft.
Builder: Edward H. Hall, Thomas E. Schull
Year: 1872
Condition: Good

Also known as Harmony Hill Bridge, this bridge was built in 1872 at Gibson's Ford by Edward H. Hall and Thomas E. Schull for $2,666. The bridge has horizontal-clapboard siding and interesting stepped portals.

Larkin Bridge

Location: Located in Marsh Creek State Park in Upper Uwchlan Township.

Stream: branch of Marsh Creek
Ownership: State
Truss type: Burr
Length: 60 ft.

Width: 14.5 ft.
Builder: Menander Wood, Ferdinand Wood
Year: 1881
Condition: Poor

The Larkin Bridge today is located over a branch of Marsh Creek within the Marsh Creek State Park. It was moved to its present location and placed on concrete abutments following the creation of the Marsh Creek dam in 1972. The original site on Marsh Creek, near the Jesse Larkin gristmill (formerly the Richard Bicking paper mill), is now under sixty feet of water. This is the second Larkin bridge. The first bridge, built in 1854, was rebuilt in 1881 by the Wood brothers.

Hall's, Sheeder Bridge

Location: On S.R. 1028 south of Sheeder in West Vincent and East Vincent townships.

Stream: French Creek
Ownership: State
Truss type: Burr
Length: 100 ft., 2 spans

Width: 15 ft.
Builder: Robert Russell, Jacob Fox
Year: 1850
Condition: Good

Bridging East and West Vincent townships, the Hall's, Sheeder Bridge is the oldest covered bridge still standing in Chester County. Its stepped portals and horizontal-clapboard siding are similar to the Wertz's or Red Covered Bridge of Berks County. Built by Robert Russell and Jacob Fox, the entire two-span bridge cost $1,564.

Kennedy Bridge

Location: On S.R. 4001 on Seven Stars Road, northwest of Kimbertown in East Vincent Township.

Stream: French Creek	**Width:** 14 ft.
Ownership: County	**Builder:** Alex King, Jesse King
Truss type: Burr	**Year:** 1856, 1986
Length: 100 ft.	**Condition:** Good

This 100-foot bridge carries the inscription, "Built for Newton Nichols, Albert Way and Wm. G. Maitland, County Commissioners by Alex King and Jesse King, contracted July 4th, Finished Oct. 1, 1856." Named for Alexander Kennedy, a local farmer, the bridge cost a total of $2,149 to build and has an unusual portal design. It was destroyed by fire in May 1986 and totally rebuilt by the county using bongossi, a nonflammable wood from Africa.

Hall's, Sheeder Bridge

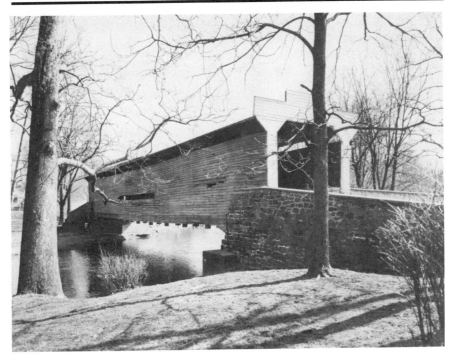
Kennedy Bridge

Rapp's Bridge

Location: On township route 463 northwest of Phoenixville in East Pikeland Township.

Stream: French Creek	**Width:** 14 ft.
Ownership: State	**Builder:** Benjamin F. Hartman
Truss type: Burr	**Year:** 1866
Length: 100 ft.	**Condition:** Good

The Rapp's Bridge was built just north of the saw and gristmills of George A. Rapp and his sons. This Burr-arch bridge has horizontal siding and its portals are embellished with boxed cornices with returns. A local carpenter built this $3,595 bridge.

Knox Bridge

Location: In Valley Forge National Historical Park, Tredyffrin Township.

Stream: Valley Creek	**Width:** 13 ft.
Ownership: Federal	**Builder:** Robert Russell
Truss type: Burr	**Year:** 1865
Length: 50 ft.	**Condition:** Good

The Knox Bridge is the second to be built on this site. The first bridge, built in 1851 by Ferdinand Wood, was destroyed by flood in 1865. This unusual bridge has horizontal siding pierced by mid-wall windows. The origin of its name is disputed, credit being given both to Philander C. Knox (1855-1921), United States Senator from Pennsylvania, and General Henry Knox (1750-1806), an officer quartered at nearby Valley Forge during the winter of 1777-1778.

LEHIGH COUNTY

Bogerts Bridge

Location: On S.R. 2010 in Little Lehigh Park, Allentown.

Stream: Little Lehigh Creek
Ownership: City
Truss type: Burr
Length: 145 ft.

Width: 15 ft.
Builder: Unknown
Year: 1841
Condition: Good

Constructed in 1841, Bogerts Bridge and Wehr's are the oldest remaining covered bridges in Lehigh County. Today this bridge has been incorporated into a city park and has been restored by the parks department. It has vertical-plank siding, gable roof and cut-stone abutments. Two concrete piers were added to help support the bridge.

Wehr's Bridge

Location: On township route 597 northwest of Stetersville in South Whitehall Township.

Stream: Jordan Creek
Ownership: County
Truss type: Burr
Length: 117 ft., 3 spans

Width: 17 ft.
Builder: Unknown
Year: 1841
Condition: Excellent

This three-span bridge has random-width horizontal siding, a gable roof and stone abutments and piers. The first few feet of the interior are covered with horizontal siding similar to the Bucks County bridges. In 1965 the bridge was strengthened by the addition of steel reinforcements.

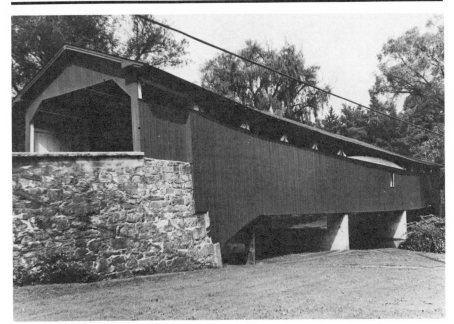

Bogerts Bridge

Wehr's Bridge

Geiger's Bridge

Schlicher's Bridge

Manasses Guth Bridge

Location: On township route 602 north of Guth in South Whitehall Township.

Stream: Jordan Creek
Ownership: County
Truss type: Burr
Length: 108 ft.

Width: 17 ft.
Builder: Unknown
Year: 1868, rebuilt 1882
Condition: Good

The unusually named bridge has horizontal clapboard siding. All of the six remaining Lehigh County covered bridges are in good condition and are all more than one hundred feet in length.

Rex's Bridge

Location: On township route 593 south of Kernsville in North Whiteland Township.

Stream: Jordan Creek
Ownership: County
Truss type: Burr
Length: 138 ft.

Width: 16 ft. 7 in.
Builder: Unknown
Year: 1858
Condition: Good

Situated between Kernsville and Weidasville, the Rex's Bridge is the longest remaining covered bridge in the county. It has narrow, horizontal clapboard siding.

Geiger's Bridge

Location: On township route 681 northwest of Weidasville in North Whitehall Township.

Stream: Jordan Creek
Ownership: County
Truss type: Burr
Length: 112 ft.

Width: 16 ft. 2 in.
Builder: Unknown
Year: 1860
Condition: Good

Also located over Jordan Creek, Geiger's Bridge has vertical siding. Its unusual stepped portals make Geiger's Bridge a popular subject for photographs.

Schlicher's Bridge

Location: On S.R. 4007 south of Schnecksville in North Whitehall Township.

Stream: Jordan Creek
Ownership: State
Truss type: Burr
Length: 108 ft.

Width: 17 ft.
Builder: Unknown
Year: 1882
Condition: Good

This is the most recent of the Lehigh County covered bridges and differs in style with its vertical siding and low, broad appearance.

Kreidersville Bridge

Location: On township route 473 in Kreidersville, Allen Township.

Stream: Hokendaugua Creek
Ownership: County
Truss type: Burr
Length: 100 ft.

Width: 16 ft. 8 in.
Builder: Unknown
Year: 1840
Condition: Good

One of the oldest covered bridges in Pennsylvania, the Kreidersville Bridge is the only one remaining in Northampton County. It was built in 1840, but has been restored and strengthened by the addition of steel reinforcements. Its narrow, horizontal siding reaches to the eaves, and it has no windows, making the interior very dark.

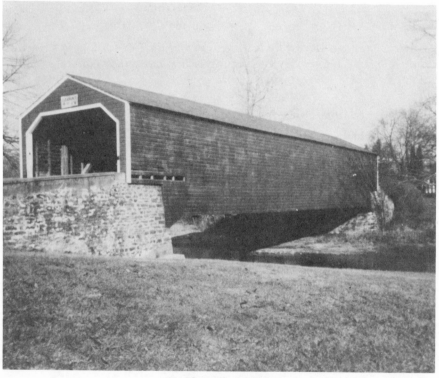

Kreidersville Bridge

Thomas Mill Bridge

Location: On Thomas Mill Road in Fairmount Park, Philadelphia.

Stream: Wissahickon Creek
Ownership: City
Truss type: Howe
Length: 86 ft. 6 in.

Width: 18 ft. 8 in.
Builder: Unknown
Year: 1855, rebuilt 1939
Condition: Good

The Thomas Mill Bridge is the oldest and largest of Pennsylvania's four remaining Howe-truss covered bridges and the only covered bridge in Philadelphia County. Its portals have unusual saw-tooth decorations.

▲▲▲▲▲▲▲▲▲▲▲▲▲▲▲▲▲▲▲▲▲▲▲▲▲▲▲▲▲▲

Northeast
R·E·G·I·O·N

Two separate river systems drain this area of Pennsylvania, the Susquehanna River to the west and the Delaware River to the east. Columbia County has the most remaining bridges in this region, with an almost equal number of Burr-arch and queenpost-truss bridges. Many covered bridges once crossed the Delaware River between Pennsylvania and New Jersey. The last wooden span over the Delaware was destroyed by flood in 1955.

This region has only a few covered bridges today. The Bradford and Sullivan County bridges, because of their settings, are some of the most attractive in the state.

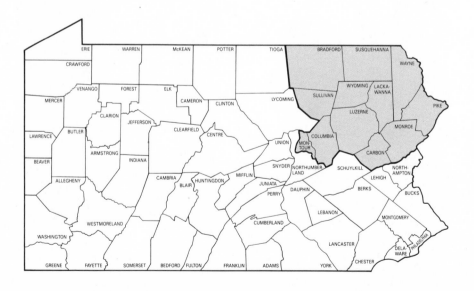

Knapp's, Luthers Mills Bridge

Location: On township route 554 northeast of Luthers Mills in Burlington Township.

Stream: Browns Creek
Ownership: County
Truss type: Burr
Length: 95 ft.

Width: 14 ft.
Builder: Unknown
Year: 1853
Condition: Excellent

Bradford County's only covered bridge spans Browns Creek and is the highest-above-water covered bridge in Pennsylvania, with a drop to the creek of more than thirty feet.

Knapp's, Luthers Mills Bridge

Harrity Bridge

Location: Next to the Beltzville Dam Park office in Franklin Township.

Stream: not over stream at present
Ownership: County
Truss type: Kingpost
Length: 87 ft.

Width: 13 ft.
Builder: Paul Buck
Year: 1841
Condition: Good

The Harrity Bridge was moved by the U.S. Army Corps of Engineers in 1970 from its original location over the Pohopoco Creek, which was flooded by the development of the Beltzville Dam. Harrity Bridge has horizontal-plank siding of mid-wall level, leaving the upper trussing open. Its gable roof is covered by wooden shingles.

Little Gap Bridge

Little Gap Bridge

Location: On township route 376 south of Little Gap in Towamensing Township.

Stream: Aquashicola Creek
Ownership: County
Truss type: Burr
Length: 73 ft.

Width: 15 ft.
Builder: Unknown
Year: c. 1860
Condition: Good

One of the two remaining covered bridges in Carbon County, the Little Gap Bridge's portals are extended from the trussing system by low walls and large, open windows.

COLUMBIA/NORTHUMBERLAND COUNTIES

Richards Bridge

Location: On township route 804 east of Elysburg between Cleveland Township, Columbia County, and Ralpho Township, Northumberland County.

Stream: South Branch, Roaring Creek
Ownership: Two counties
Truss type: modified Queenpost
Length: 54 ft.

Width: 11 ft.
Builder: Obediah S. Campbell
Year: 1852
Condition: Good

This bridge was built in 1852 by Obediah S. Campbell, who used a subdivided Howe truss with a queenpost added for increased capacity. It appears that the builder altered the truss style to match his own preference.

Krickbaum Bridge

Location: On township route 459 east of Elysburg between Cleveland Township, Columbia County, and Ralpho Township, Northumberland County.

Stream: South Branch, Roaring Creek
Ownership: Two counties
Truss type: Queenpost
Length: 51 ft.

Width: 13 ft. 8 in.
Builder: George W. Keefer
Year: 1876
Condition: Good

This bridge is a single span utilizing a queenpost trussing system. Its high board-and-batten sidewalls leave only narrow window openings under the eaves, making the bridge interior very dark.

Krickbaum Bridge

Lawrence L. Knoebel Bridge

Lawrence L. Knoebel Bridge

Location: In the Knoebel's Grove Campground between Cleveland Township, Columbia County, and Ralpho Township, Northumberland County.

Stream: South Branch, Roaring Creek
Ownership: Private
Truss type: Queenpost
Length: 40 ft.

Width: 15 ft.
Builder: Unknown
Year: 1875
Condition: Good

The covered bridge at Knoebel's Grove was built in 1875 over West Creek near Benton. When road relocation by-passed the bridge in 1936, it was sold. The bridge was carefully dismantled, moved the fifty miles to the Grove, and reconstructed. This bridge has a side-covered walkway; only one other bridge in Pennsylvania has such a sidewall.

COLUMBIA COUNTY

(See also Columbia/Northumberland Counties)

Fowlersville Bridge

Location: Off S.R. 1017 east of Evansville in Briar Creek Township.

Stream: Crosses small run
Ownership: County
Truss type: Queenpost
Length: 40 ft.

Width: 15 ft.
Builder: Charles King
Year: 1886
Condition: Good

This short queenpost-truss bridge has board-and-batten siding. One of the last covered bridges built in the county, the Fowlersville Bridge was built at a cost of $397 and named for the Fowler family who settled in the area after the Revolutionary War. This bridge was relocated to Briar Creek Lake Park from its original location on the West Branch, Briar Creek.

Shoemaker Bridge

Location: On S.R. 4027 near route 422, northwest of Iola in Pine Township.

Stream: West Branch Run
Ownership: County
Truss type: Queenpost
Length: 38 ft.

Width: 15 ft.
Builder: T. S. Christian
Year: 1881
Condition: Good

Built in 1881, the Shoemaker Bridge was named after a local farmer and lumberman, Joseph Shoemaker. One of the bridge's sidewalls is shorter because the road curves sharply at the foot of the mountain.

Sam Eckman Bridge

Location: On township route 548 north of Millville and Iola, between Pine and Greenwood townships.

Stream: Little Fishing Creek
Ownership: County
Truss type: Warren
Length: 53 ft.

Width: 14 ft. 6 in.
Builder: Joseph Redline
Year: 1876
Condition: Good

This bridge was built for $498 and named for a local farmer who also operated a shingle mill and burch-oil factory nearby. This bridge is one of two Warren-truss covered bridges in Pennsylvania; the other is also in Columbia County.

Fowlersville Bridge

Josiah Hess Bridge

Location: On township route 563 between Forks and Jonestown in Fishing Creek Township.

Stream: Huntington Creek
Ownership: County
Truss type: Burr
Length: 105 ft. 2 in.

Width: 15 ft. 5 in.
Builder: Joseph Redline
Year: 1875
Condition: Good

Constructed in 1875 at a cost of $1,349.50, the Josiah Hess Bridge is a Burr-truss bridge with five diagonal braces on each side of the central kingpost. It was named after the Hess family who owned a sawmill and farm nearby.

East and West Paden Bridges (Twin Bridge)

East Paden Bridge (Twin Bridge)

Location: On S.R. 1020 east of Forks in Fishing Creek Township.

Stream: Huntington Creek
Ownership: County
Truss type: Queenpost
Length: 59 ft.

Width: 15 ft.
Builder: W. C. Pennington
Year: 1884
Condition: Good

One of the Twin Bridges, it was constructed in 1884 by W. C. Pennington at a cost of $720. The two bridges were named for a local sawmiller, John Paden. This bridge is closed to traffic.

West Paden Bridge (Twin Bridge)

Location: On S.R. 1020 east of Forks in Fishing Creek Township.

Stream: Huntington Creek
Ownership: County
Truss type: Burr
Length: 77 ft.

Width: 15 ft.
Builder: W. C. Pennington
Year: 1884
Condition: Good

West Paden is the second of the "Twin Bridges" built by W. C. Pennington. The name "Twin Bridges" comes from their location end-to-end, rather than their truss type or identical styles. This bridge is closed to traffic.

Welle Hess, Laubach Bridge

Location: Was located between Grassmere Park and Laubach in Sugarloaf Township.

Stream: Fishing Creek
Ownership: State
Truss type: Burr
Length: 126 ft.

Width: 15 ft.
Builder: Clinton Cole, Montgomery Cole
Year: 1871

This was the second bridge on the site. The first bridge was destroyed by the flood of July, 1848. This bridge collapsed on July 19, 1981.

Snyder Bridge

Location: On township route 361 east of Slabtown in Locust Township.

Stream: North Branch, Roaring Creek
Ownership: County
Truss type: Queenpost
Length: 41 ft.

Width: 14 ft. 9 in.
Builder: Unknown
Year: 1900
Condition: Good

Named for its location near the John Snyder gristmill, this bridge has vertical-plank siding and open windows under the eaves. Little is known of its history.

Wagner Bridge

Location: Was located north of Newlin and Mill Grove in Locust Township.

Stream: North Branch, Roaring Creek
Ownership: County
Truss type: Queenpost
Length: 56 ft. 5 in.

Width: 14 ft.
Builder: A. J. Knoebel
Year: 1874
Condition: Fair

The second bridge on the site, the Wagner Bridge was built by A. J. Knoebel in 1874 at a total cost of $849.50. Its walls are vertical board-and-batten and its floor consists of horizontal boards covered with vertical boards and two runways over them. The covered bridge has been replaced, being carefully dismantled for later reconstruction.

Davis Bridge

Location: On township route 356 south of Catawissa and west of Queen City in Cleveland Township.

Stream: North Branch, Roaring Creek
Ownership: County
Truss type: Burr
Length: 87 ft. 1 in.

Width: 14 ft. 2 in.
Builder: Daniel Kostenbauder
Year: 1875
Condition: Fair

Built at a cost of $1,248, this bridge was named for a nearby farmer.

Wanich Bridge

Location: On township route 493 north of Fernville and Bloomsburg in Hemlock and Mt. Pleasant townships.

Stream: Little Fishing Creek
Ownership: County
Truss type: Burr
Length: 78 ft.

Width: 15 ft. 3 in.
Builder: George Russell, Jr.
Year: 1884
Condition: Excellent

The Wanich Bridge was named for a local farmer, John Wanich. This bridge has horizontal siding and a tarred metal roof covered with wooden shingles. The road surface is laid in a diagonal pattern, with runways. The original stone-and-mortar abutments have been repaired with concrete only where needed. No steel reinforcements have been used in the undergirding of the deck.

Furnace Bridge

Location: On township route 373 south of Catawissa in Cleveland Township.

Stream: North Branch, Roaring Creek
Ownership: County
Truss type: Queenpost
Length: 90 ft.

Width: 13 ft. 4 in.
Builder: C. W. Eves
Year: 1882
Condition: Good

Built at a cost of $1,044.75, the Furnace Bridge is the longest queenpost-truss bridge in Pennsylvania. The use of queenpost trussing is usually restricted to bridges of sixty to seventy feet.

Stillwater Bridge

Location: On township route 629 in Stillwater.

Stream: Big Fishing Creek
Ownership: County
Truss type: Burr
Length: 127 ft.

Width: 15 ft. 3 in.
Builder: James McHenry
Year: 1849
Condition: Good

One of the longest bridges in Columbia County, the Stillwater Bridge was built at a cost of $1,124. Its sidewalls are covered with vertical boards in board-and-batten style. This bridge is closed to traffic.

"Y" Bridge

Location: Was located on township route 757 near Central in Sugarloaf Township.

Stream: East Branch, Fishing Creek
Ownership: County
Truss type: Queenpost

Length: 76 ft.
Width: 14 ft.
Builder: J. M. Larish
Year: 1887

One of Columbia County's twelve queenpost-truss covered bridges, it was probably named for the nearby "Y" formation of the railroad tracks used for turning trains back into Bloomsburg. This bridge was destroyed by fire.

Kramer Bridge

Location: On township route 572 southwest of Rohrsburg in Greenwood Township.

Stream: Mud Run
Ownership: County
Truss type: Queenpost
Length: 39 ft.

Width: 13 ft. 8 in.
Builder: C. W. Eves
Year: 1881
Condition: Good

Named for a local farmer, Alexander Kramer, this bridge cost $414.50 to construct in 1881. Its sidewalls are board and batten and its deck is covered with horizontal boards, with two runways.

Jud Christian Bridge

Location: On township route 685 north of Millville and Iola, between Pine and Jackson townships.

Stream: Little Fishing Creek
Ownership: County
Truss type: Queenpost
Length: 43 ft.

Width: 12 ft. 8 in.
Builder: William L. Manning
Year: 1876
Condition: Excellent

Built at a cost of $239 and named for a nearby farmer and lumberman, this bridge is in near-perfect condition.

Patterson Bridge

Location: On township route 575 between Orangeville and Rohrsburg in Orange Township.

Stream: Green Creek
Ownership: County
Truss type: Burr
Length: 63 ft.

Width: 14 ft. 7 in.
Builder: Frank Derr
Year: 1875
Condition: Good

The sidewalls of this bridge are unusual in that they have side windows with movable wooden awnings which can be closed in bad weather. Named for the Patterson sawmill, which was located nearby, this bridge cost $804 to build in 1875.

Patterson Bridge

Interior, Patterson Bridge

Parr's Mill Bridge

Location: On township route 328 south of Catawissa between Franklin and Cleveland townships.

Stream: North Branch, Roaring Creek
Ownership: County
Truss type: Burr
Length: 66 ft.

Width: 12 ft. 2 in.
Builder: F. L. Shuman
Year: 1865
Condition: Good

This bridge was named for a local gristmill and has two different wall sidings. The western wall is covered with horizontal clapboard and the east wall has vertical-plank siding. As the portal ends also have the horizontal clapboard, this probably was the original wall treatment.

Rohrbach Bridge

Location: Was located southwest of Catawissa in Franklin Township.

Stream: South Branch, Roaring Creek
Ownership: County
Truss type: Queenpost
Length: 64 ft. 4 in.

Width: 14 ft. 5 in.
Builder: Joseph Fulton
Year: 1846

The Rohrbach Bridge was the oldest remaining covered bridge in Columbia County and cost only $183 to build in 1846. The William Rohrbach sawmill and lumbering business were located nearby until 1865. This bridge has been dismantled.

Rupert Bridge

Location: On township route 449 between Bloomsburg and Montour Township.

Stream: Fishing Creek
Ownership: County
Truss type: Burr
Length: 166 ft.

Width: 17 ft. 9 in.
Builder: Jesse M. Beard
Year: 1847
Condition: Good

The Rupert Bridge was named for the nearby community of Rupert. Rupert was settled in 1788 and named for Leonard Rupert. The Rupert Bridge is the longest remaining covered bridge in Columbia County.

Hollingshead Bridge

Location: On township route 422 southeast of Catawissa in Catawissa Township.

Stream: Catawissa Creek
Ownership: County
Truss type: Burr
Length: 116 ft. 10 in.

Width: 15 ft. 4 in.
Builder: Peter Ent
Year: 1850
Condition: Good

Named for a local miller, the Hollingshead Bridge has board-and-batten sidewalls and small, square windows. The builder, Peter Ent, was paid $1,180 to build this bridge in 1850.

Riegel Bridge

Location: Was located north of Rohrbach in Franklin Township.

Stream: Roaring Creek
Ownership: County
Truss type: Burr
Length: 107 ft. 3 in.

Width: 14 ft. 10 in.
Builder: Jacob Kostenbaufer
Year: 1870

This bridge was often confused with the Rishel covered bridge in Northumberland County, and was, therefore, mistakenly thought to be one of the oldest remaining covered bridges in Pennsylvania. The Riegel Bridge was built in 1870 at a cost of $1,882.50 and was named for a nearby farmer. It was destroyed by arson in 1979.

Creasyville Bridge

Location: On township route 602 north of Millville and Jackson townships.

Stream: Little Fishing Creek
Ownership: County
Truss type: Queenpost
Length: 44 ft. 6 in.

Width: 14 ft.
Builder: R. S. Christian
Year: 1881
Condition: Good

The Creasyville Bridge is one of the shortest covered bridges in Columbia County today. Its sidewalls are board-and-batten design and its flooring is laid in a herringbone pattern, with two runways. Its cost of construction in 1881 was $301.25.

Johnson Bridge

Location: On township route 320 just east of the Northumberland County boundary in Cleveland Township.

Stream: Mugser Run
Ownership: County
Truss type: Warren
Length: 51 ft.

Width: 13 ft. 6 in.
Builder: Daniel Stine
Year: 1882
Condition: Good

The Johnson Bridge is one of two Warren-truss covered bridges remaining in Pennsylvania. This short bridge cost $799 to build in 1882.

LUZERNE COUNTY

Bittenbender's Bridge

Location: On private property off S.R. 4006 south of Huntington Mills in Huntington Township.

Stream: Huntington Creek
Ownership: Private
Truss type: Queenpost
Length: 62 ft.

Width: 13 ft.
Builder: Frank Monroe, Stephen Harrison Dodson
Year: 1888
Condition: Fair

Bittenbender's Bridge, located over Huntington Creek, is the last covered bridge in Luzerne County. This queenpost-truss bridge is in fair condition, with repairs having been made in 1936 by the addition of a center concrete pier and undergirding. Its rough vertical-plank siding is missing in several places. In 1927 this bridge was almost burned when the Ku Klux Klan burned the two Bittenbender barns.

Bittenbender's Bridge

Gottlieb Brown, Sam Wagner Bridge

Location: On township route 308 east of Potts Grove between East Chillisquaque Township, Northumberland County, and Liberty Township, Montour County.

Stream: Chillisquaque Creek
Ownership: Two counties
Truss type: Burr
Length: 78 ft.

Width: 15 ft.
Builder: George W. Keefer
Year: 1881
Condition: Good

This bridge was built in 1881 by George W. Keefer near the old Gottlieb Brown farm at a total cost of $939 and utilizes the Burr-arch trussing system. It has vertical-plank siding and its stone abutments have been capped with concrete.

Gottlieb Brown, Sam Wagner Bridge

Keefer Bridge

MONTOUR COUNTY

(See also Montour/Northumberland Counties)

Keefer Bridge

Location: On township route 346 southwest of Washingtonville in Liberty Township.

Stream: Chillisquaque Creek
Ownership: County
Truss type: Burr
Length: 75 ft.

Width: 15 ft.
Builder: William Butler
Year: 1853, 1983
Condition: Good

The Keefer Bridge was built in 1853 at a cost of $498 near the Geringer Mill, no longer existent. This bridge has an unusual square portal design not common in Pennsylvania. In 1983, this bridge was rebuilt by the county at the same location.

Forksville Bridge

Location: On a spur of S.R. 4012 at Forksville in Forks Township.

Stream: Loyalsock Creek
Ownership: State
Truss type: Burr
Length: 130 ft.

Width: 15 ft.
Builder: Sadler Rodgers
Year: 1850
Condition: Good

This large, one-span bridge crosses Loyalsock Creek and serves the small community of Forksville. Set over the rocky Loyalsock Creek, the Forksville Bridge has one of the most attractive settings in the state. The bridge itself is typical with its vertical-plank siding and gable roof.

Forksville Bridge

Hillsgrove Bridge

Location: On township route 357 northeast of Hillsgrove in Elkland Township.

Stream: Loyalsock Creek
Ownership: County
Truss type: Burr
Length: 152 ft.

Width: 18 ft.
Builder: Sadler Rodgers
Year: c. 1850
Condition: Good

Hillsgrove Bridge crosses Loyalsock Creek south of the Forksville Bridge. This and the Forksville Bridge are similar in design and were built by the same builder. Set against the hillside, the Hillsgrove Bridge has vertical-plank siding and narrow-width laid flooring.

Sonestown Bridge

Sonestown Bridge

Location: On township route 310 south of Sonestown in Davidson Township.

Stream: Muncy Creek
Ownership: County
Truss type: Burr
Length: 102 ft.

Width: 15 ft.
Builder: Unknown
Year: c. 1850
Condition: Good

Sonestown Bridge crosses Muncy Creek in eastern Sullivan County. Built to reach Johnny Hazen's gristmill, the bridge has vertical-plank siding, with a panel of windows under the eaves. Its flooring is wide planks laid widthwise with vertically laid runners.

North Central

R·E·G·I·O·N

The covered bridges of this region are clustered in the southern counties drained by the Susquehanna River. Examples of the three major trussing systems, Burr, kingpost and queenpost, can be seen in this region.

The McGees Mill Bridge in Clearfield County is the sole remaining wooden span crossing a main branch of the Susquehanna River.

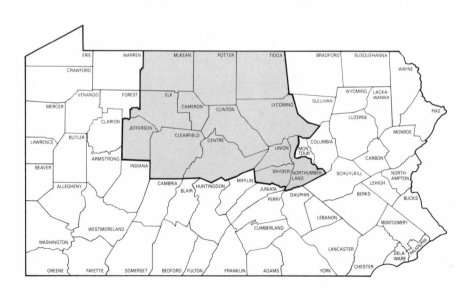

CLEARFIELD COUNTY

McGees Mills Bridge

McGees Mills Bridge

Location: On township route 322 in McGees Mills, Bell Township.

Stream: West Branch, Susquehanna River

Ownership: County

Truss type: Burr

Length: 116 ft.

Width: 15 ft.

Builder: Thomas McGee

Year: 1873

Condition: Good

The McGees Mills Bridge is a single-span bridge with horizontal siding, a shingle-covered gable roof, and cut-stone abutments. The interior has been encased with protective wooden walls, and the floor boards are narrow and horizontally laid. This is the only covered bridge left in Clearfield County.

Logan Mill Bridge

Location: On S.R. 2007 at Logan Mills, Logan Township.

Stream: Fishing Creek
Ownership: State
Truss type: Queenpost
Length: 55 ft.

Width: 12 ft.
Builder: Unknown
Year: 1874
Condition: Fair

The Logan Mill Bridge is the only remaining covered bridge in the county in an area once rich in these covered spans. This bridge is an unusual example of the queenpost trussing system with its unusually shallow queenpost truss of only six to eight feet. The shallowness of the trusses would tend to make the bridge rather unstable, and it has been propped with wooden braces between the creek bed and bridge floor.

Logan Mill Bridge

North Oriental, Beaver Bridge

Location: On S.R. 2026 north of Oriental between Susquehanna Township, Juniata County, and Perry Township, Snyder County.

Stream: Mahantango Creek
Ownership: State
Truss type: Kingpost
Length: 62 ft.

Width: 12 ft. 6 in.
Builder: Unknown
Year: 1908
Condition: Good

The North Oriental Bridge has vertical siding and a tin-covered gable roof. This bridge has been braced mid-stream to help support its trussing system. However, it was damaged in 1985 and rebuilt in 1987.

North Oriental, Beaver Bridge

East Oriental, Shaeffer Bridge

Location: On S.R. 2026 east of Oriental between Susquehanna Township, Juniata County, and Perry Township, Snyder County.

Stream: Mahantango Creek
Ownership: Private
Truss type: Burr
Length: 108 ft.

Width: 15 ft. 6 in.
Builder: Unknown
Year: 1907
Condition: Fair

The East Oriental Bridge has very large, cut-stone abutments, vertical-plank siding and a tin-covered gable roof.

LYCOMING COUNTY

Buttonwood Bridge

Location: On township route 816 north of Buttonwood in Jackson Township.

Stream: Block House Creek
Ownership: County
Truss type: Burr
Length: 57 ft.

Width: 14 ft. 5 in.
Builder: Unknown
Year: 1898
Condition: Good

Located just north of the community of Buttonwood in a broad valley, the Buttonwood Bridge serves several small farms. This Burr-arch bridge is in very good condition and its truss reaches to eave level.

Cogan House Bridge

Location: Off township route 784 southwest of Cogan House in Cogan House Township.

Stream: Larrys Creek
Ownership: County
Truss type: Burr
Length: 81 ft.

Width: 19 ft. 7 in.
Builder: Unknown
Year: 1877
Condition: Good

Located in a remote valley, the Cogan House Bridge services township route 816, a dirt road serving private land and state game land. This is the oldest and longest covered bridge remaining in the county. Its rough, horizontal siding and wooden shingles help this bridge blend into the surrounding forest.

Cogan House Bridge

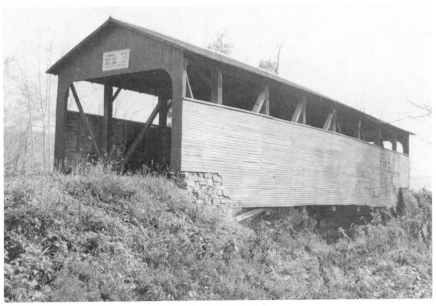

Lairdsville, Frazier Bridge

Lairdsville, Frazier Bridge

Location: On township route 664 north of Opp in Moreland Township.

Stream: Little Muncy Creek
Ownership: County
Truss type: Burr
Length: 60 ft.

Width: 15 ft. 1 in.
Builder: Unknown
Year: 1888
Condition: Fair

Located in a broad valley, the Lairdsville Bridge serves several farms on township route 664, a dirt road. Stone abutments support this Burr-arch structure. Its gable roof is tin covered, and its sides are three-fourths horizontal-siding covered, leaving an open panel under the eaves for light.

NORTHUMBERLAND COUNTY

(See also Montour/Northumberland Counties)

Keefer Station Bridge

Location: On township route 698 east of Sunbury in Upper Augusta Township.

Stream: Shamokin Creek
Ownership: County
Truss type: Burr
Length: 109 ft.

Width: 14 ft. 1 in.
Builder: George W. Keefer
Year: 1888
Condition: Good

The Keefer Station Bridge was built by George W. Keefer in 1888 near the farm of John G. Bright, at a cost of $882. This bridge has unusual overhanging portals and vertical-plank siding.

Rishel Bridge

Location: On township route 573, east of Montandon between West Chillisquaque and East Chillisquaque townships.

Stream: Chillisquaque Creek
Ownership: County
Truss type: Burr
Length: 96 ft.

Width: 17 ft. 3 in.
Builder: John Shriner, Jr., Zacheus
   Braley
Year: 1830
Condition: Good

The Rishel Bridge is thought by some to be the oldest remaining covered bridge in Pennsylvania. It has high, vertical-plank sidewalls with a narrow panel of windows under the eaves.

Keefer Station Bridge

Interior, Rishel Bridge

Himmel's Church Bridge

Himmel's Church Bridge

Location: On township route 442 northeast of Rebuck in Washington Township.

Stream: Schwaben Creek
Ownership: County
Truss type: Kingpost
Length: 33 ft.

Width: 15 ft.
Builder: Peter Keefer
Year: 1874
Condition: Good

This short bridge utilizes the kingpost trussing system and has low, vertical-plank sidewalls, which leave large window panels under the eaves.

(See also Juniata/Snyder Counties)

Dreese's, Beavertown Bridge

Location: On township route 600 northwest of Beavertown in Beaver Township.

Stream: Middle Creek
Ownership: County
Truss type: Burr
Length: 95 ft.

Width: 14 ft. 8 in.
Builder: Unknown
Year: c. 1870
Condition: Good

Dreese's Bridge has vertical siding, a gable roof and triangular-shaped portals. The bridge has been by-passed.

Dreese's, Beavertown Bridge

Aline, Meiserville Bridge

Klinepeter's, Gross Bridge

Location: Spans floodway in Beaver Springs in Spring Township.

Stream: Middle Creek
Ownership: County
Truss type: Burr
Length: 100 ft.

Width: 16 ft. 4 in.
Builder: Unknown
Year: c. 1871
Condition: Good

Klinepeter's Bridge is identical in styling to the Dresse's Bridge to the east.

Aline, Meiserville Bridge

Location: 4.2 miles south of intersection of route 35 and route 104 in Perry Township.

Stream: North Branch, Mahan-tango Creek
Ownership: Township
Truss type: Burr
Length: 33 ft.

Width: 18 ft.
Builder: Unknown
Year: 1884
Condition: Good

Aline Bridge has vertical-plank siding and triangular-shaped portal openings. This short Burr-arch bridge is in good condition. It was by-passed in 1982 and is now closed to vehicular traffic.

116

Millmont Red Bridge

Location: On township route 320 southwest of Millmont in Hartley Township.

Stream: Penns Creek
Ownership: County
Truss type: Burr
Length: 142 ft.

Width: 14 ft.
Builder: Unknown
Year: 1855
Condition: Good

This long covered bridge is unusual in its styling, with its horizontal, narrow clapboards and in-sloping portals.

Hayes Bridge

Location: On township route 376 east of Hartleton in West Buffalo Township.

Stream: Buffalo Creek
Ownership: County
Truss type: Kingpost
Length: 60 ft.

Width: 16 ft.
Builder: Unknown
Year: 1882
Condition: Good

Set high on cut-stone abutments, the Hayes Bridge has vertical-plank siding and a gable roof with wide overhanging eaves.

Milmont Red Bridge

Hassenplug Bridge

Hassenplug Bridge

Location: On North Fourth Street in Mifflinburg.

Stream: Buffalo Creek	**Width:** 16 ft.
Ownership: County	**Builder:** Unknown
Truss type: Burr	**Year:** 1825, rebuilt 1959
Length: 70 ft.	**Condition:** Good

This bridge was named after the Hassenplug family, who were local farmers. In recent years the county has removed the original floor and replaced it with an open steel deck.

Factory, Horsham Bridge

Location: On township route 526 west of White Deer in White Deer Township.

Stream: White Deer Creek	**Width:** 16 ft.
Ownership: County	**Builder:** Unknown
Truss type: Kingpost, Queenpost	**Year:** 1880
Length: 60 ft.	**Condition:** Good

Built to serve early woolen mills which once stood nearby, the Factory Bridge has vertical-plank siding and triangular-shaped portals. The original wooden floor has been covered with asphalt.

Lewisburg Penitentiary Bridge

Location: Off S.R. 1002 southeast of Kelly Point between Kelly and Buffalo townships.

Stream: Little Buffalo Creek
Ownership: Federal
Truss type: Kingpost, Queenpost
Length: 33 ft.

Width: 15 ft.
Builder: Unknown
Year: 1850
Condition: Good

Located on the penitentiary grounds, this short covered bridge has wide horizontal-clapboard siding. This bridge is closed to the public.

Lewisburg Penitentiary Bridge

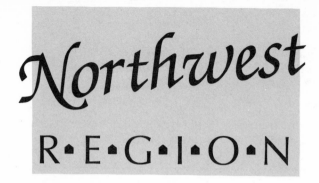

Northwest
R·E·G·I·O·N

Drained by the Lake Erie watershed in the north and the Ohio watershed in the south, this region has only seven remaining covered bridges. Pennsylvania's only Smith-truss covered bridge is located in this region in Mercer County.

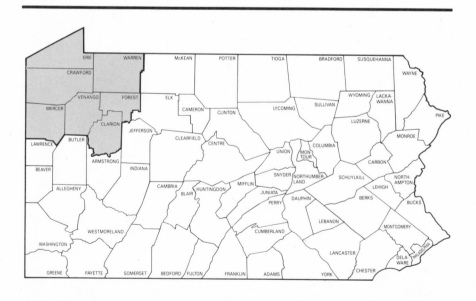

Harrington Bridge

Location: On S.R. 3003 northeast of Cherry Hill between Springfield and Conneaut townships.

Stream: West Branch, Conneaut Creek
Ownership: State
Truss type: Kingpost
Length: 72 ft.

Width: 14 ft.
Builder: William Sherman
Year: c. 1870
Condition: Good

This multiple kingpost-truss bridge has vertical siding and cut-stone abutments. Its gable roof is covered with wooden shingles. The plain portal slopes inward toward the trussing system.

Gudgeonville Bridge

Gudgeonville Bridge

Location: On township route 400 southeast of Girard in Girard Township.

Stream: Elk Creek
Ownership: Township
Truss type: Kingpost
Length: 72 ft.

Width: 14 ft.
Builder: William Sherman
Year: 1868
Condition: Fair

The Gudgeonville Bridge is one of the most spectacular covered bridges in the state because of its location. Crossing Elk Creek in a deep valley, the bridge is a beautiful view in all seasons. Like Harrington, the Gudgeonville Bridge has narrow vertical siding.

Waterford Bridge

Location: On township route 459 just east of Waterford in Waterford Township.

Stream: LeBoeuf Creek
Ownership: Township
Truss type: Town
Length: 78 ft.

Width: 15 ft.
Builder: Richard Cross, architect;
　　Charles & James Phelps, builders
Year: 1875
Condition: Good

Located just outside the small community of Waterford, this covered bridge uses the Town lattice-trussing system. Today, Pennsylvania has only seventeen Town-truss covered bridges.

Carman Bridge

Location: On township route 686 northeast of Cherry Hill between Springfield and Conneaut townships.

Stream: Conneaut Creek
Ownership: Township
Truss type: Kingpost
Length: 75 ft.

Width: 14 ft.
Builder: William Sherman
Year: c. 1870
Condition: Fair

Like the Harrington and Gudgeonville bridges, the Carman Bridge was built by William Sherman and is identical in style with its narrow vertical siding, gable roof, and cut-stone abutments. Painted above the north portal is an advertisement for Stines & Wingate Clothing, a department store in nearby Conneaut, Ohio, which went out of business eighty years ago.

Carman Bridge

LAWRENCE COUNTY

McConnell's Mill Bridge

Location: On township route 415, McConnells Mill in Slippery Rock Township.

Stream: Slippery Rock Creek
Ownership: County
Truss type: Howe
Length: 96 ft.

Width: 15 ft.
Builder: Unknown
Year: 1874
Condition: Good

McConnell's Mill Bridge is one of the four remaining Howe-truss bridges in Pennsylvania, and is the longest of the four. The bridge is in very good condition and located near the mill for which it was named. This area is maintained as a state park today.

Banks Bridge

Location: On township route 476 southwest of Volant, Wilmington Township.

Stream: Neshannock Creek
Ownership: County
Truss type: Burr
Length: 121 ft.

Width: 15 ft.
Builder: Unknown
Year: 1889
Condition: Good

Lawrence County has only two covered bridges remaining. The Banks Bridge was built in the year 1889 and uses the Burr-arch trussing system. This long bridge is similar in styling to Bucks County bridges, with its interior walls to protect the trusses.

McConnell's Mill Bridge

Kidd's Mill Bridge

Location: On township route 471 southeast of Shenango in Pymatuning Township.

Stream: Shenango River
Ownership: County
Truss type: Smith
Length: 114 ft.

Width: 15 ft.
Builder: Unknown
Year: 1868
Condition: Good

The Kidd's Mill Bridge is the only remaining example of the Smith truss in the eastern United States. This truss type was developed by Robert Smith of Tippecanoe City, Ohio.

Kidd's Mill Bridge

PHOTO CREDITS

Cover: Packsaddle Bridge, Somerset County; Isaac Geib, Grant Heilman Photography

Camelback Bridge, Harrisburg, Dauphin County; J. Horace McFarland, PHMC files

Adams County	Heikes Bridge	S. M. Zacher
	Sauck's Bridge	T. Harrison
Bedford County	Raystown Bridge	S. M. Zacher
	Colvin Bridge	Bedford Co. Survey
	Claycomb Bridge	Bedford Co. Survey
	McDaniels Bridge	Bedford Co. Survey
Berks County	Wertz's Bridge	M. Stuart
	Dreibelbis Bridge	G. Brinton
	Pleasantville Bridge	G. Brinton
	Greisemer's Mill Bridge	G. Brinton
Bradford County	Knapp's Bridge	S. M. Zacher
Bucks County	Loux Bridge	S. M. Zacher
	Van Sant Bridge	S. M. Zacher
	Haupt's Mill Bridge	S. M. Zacher
	South Perkasie Bridge	S. M. Zacher
	Erwinna Bridge	S. M. Zacher
Carbon County	Little Gap Bridge	J. Nester
Chester/Delaware Counties	Bartram's Bridge	W. W. Pryse
Chester County	Speakman No. 2 Bridge	S. M. Zacher
	Kennedy Bridge	PHMC files
	Hall's, Sheeder Bridge	PHMC files
Clearfield County	McGees Mills Bridge	M. Riley
Clinton County	Logan Mill Bridge	R. E. Menne AD/ART/Photo Service
Columbia/ Northumberland Counties	Krickbaum Bridge	Columbia County Planning Commission
	Lawrence L. Knoebel Bridge	R. E. Menne AD/ART/Photo Service
Columbia County	Fowlersville Bridge	Columbia County Tourist Promotion Agency
	Patterson Bridge	
	Twin Bridges	PHMC files
Cumberland County	Thompson's Bridge	S. M. Zacher
Dauphin County	Henninger Farm Bridge	S. M. Zacher
	Everhart Bridge	S. M. Zacher
Franklin County	Martin's Mill Bridge	PHMC files
Greene County	Grimes Bridge	Washington & Greene County Tourist Promotion Agency
	King Bridge	
	Neddie Woods Bridge	
	Carmichaels Bridge	
	Scott Bridge	
Huntingdon County	St. Mary's Bridge	Pa. Department of Transportation

Indiana County	Kintersburg Bridge	S. M. Zacher
	Trussal Bridge	S. M. Zacher
Juniata County	Lehmans Bridge	T. Casner Gilson
Juniata/Snyder Counties	North Oriental Bridge	R. E. Menne AD/ART/Photo Service
Lancaster County	Pool Forge Bridge	S. M. Zacher
	Herr's Mill Bridge	S. M. Zacher
	Erb's Bridge	S. M. Zacher
	Zook's Mill Bridge	S. M. Zacher
	Schenck's Mill Bridge	S. M. Zacher
Lawrence County	McConnell's Mill Bridge	J. Landolfi
Lehigh County	Schlichers Bridge	S. M. Zacher
	Geigers Bridge	E. Gramportone
	Wehr's Bridge	E. Gramportone
	Bogert's Bridge	E. Gramportone
Luzerne County	Bittenbenders Bridge	A. Bohlin
Lycoming County	Lairdsville Bridge	S. M. Zacher
	Cogan House Bridge	S. M. Zacher
Mercer County	Kidd's Mill Bridge	PHMC files

Montour/
  Northumberland
  Counties
	Gottlieb Brown Bridge	PHMC files

Montour County	Keefer Bridge	R. E. Menne AD/ART/Photo Service
Northampton County	Kreidersville Bridge	PHMC files
Northumberland County	Rishel Bridge	R. E. Menne
	Himmel's Bridge	AD/ART/Photo Service
	Keefers Station Bridge	
Perry County	New Germantown Bridge	S. M. Zacher
	Adairs Bridge	S. M. Zacher
	Mt. Pleasant Bridge	S. M. Zacher
	Waggoner's Bridge	S. M. Zacher
	Book's Bridge	S. M. Zacher
Schuylkill County	Zimmerman's Bridge	Schuylkill Co.
Snyder County	Aline Bridge	R. E. Menne
	Dreese Bridge	AD/ART/Photo Service
Somerset County	Walter's Mill Bridge	Somerset County
	Beechdale Bridge	Historical Society
	Barronvale Bridge	
	Packsaddle Bridge	
	Glessner Bridge	
	New Baltimore Bridge	
	King's Bridge	
Sullivan County	Forksville Bridge	S. M. Zacher
	Sonestown Bridge	S. M. Zacher
Union County	Millmont Red Bridge	C. M. Snyder
	Lewisburg Penitentiary Bridge	R. E. Menne
	Hassenplug Bridge	AD/ART/Photo Service

Washington/Greene Counties	Davis Bridge	Washington & Greene County Tourist Promotion Agency
Washington County	Devil's Den Bridge Wyit Sprowls Bridge Jackson Mill Bridge Bailey Bridge	Washington & Greene County Tourist Promotion Agency
Westmoreland County	Bells Mills Bridge	S. M. Zacher

BIBLIOGRAPHY

Allen, Richard Sanders. *Covered Bridges of the Middle Atlantic States*. Brattleboro, Vermont: Stephen Greene Press, 1959.

Columbia-Montour Joint Planning Commission. *Columbia and Montour Historic Transportation Study*. Joint Planning Commission, June 1976.

James, Arthur E. *Covered Bridges of Chester County, Pennsylvania*. West Chester: Chester County Historical Society, 1976.

Lane, Oscar F., ed. *World Guide to Covered Bridges*. The National Society for the Preservation of Covered Bridges, Inc., Revised, April 1, 1972.

Smith, Elmer L. *Covered Bridges of Pennsylvania Dutchland*. Akron, Pennsylvania: Applied Arts Publishers, 1960.

Statewide Covered Bridge Assessment for the Pennsylvania Department of Transportation. Oretega Consulting, Media, Pennsylvania, 1991.

INDEX

Pine Valley Bridge	38-09-12	18	4461440	484040	72
Twining Ford Bridge	38-09-13	18	4452410	503000	73

CARBON COUNTY

Harrity Bridge	38-13-01	18	4523080	446000	88
Little Gap Bridge	38-13-02	18	4519940	455920	89

CHESTER/DELAWARE COUNTIES

Bartram's Bridge	38-15-17 38-23-02	18	4426510	462640	74

CHESTER COUNTY

Rudolph & Arthur Bridge	38-15-01	18	4399700	424380	74
Glen Hope Bridge	38-15-02	18	4397630	422200	75
Linton Stevens Bridge	38-15-03	18	4400920	421810	75
Speakman No. 1 Bridge	38-15-05	18	4420030	429680	75
Speakman No. 2, Mary Ann Pyle Bridge	38-15-06	18	4419180	431610	76
Hayes Clark Bridge	38-15-07	18	4419000	431730	76
Gibson's Bridge	38-15-10	18	4425120	441660	77
Larkin Bridge	38-15-11	18	4435670	438540	77
Hall's, Sheeder Bridge	38-15-12	18	4444100	447100	77
Kennedy Bridge	38-15-13	18	4443270	450860	78
Rapp's Bridge	38-15-14	18	4443150	453740	79
Knox Bridge	38-15-15	18	4437320	461070	79

CLEARFIELD COUNTY

McGees Mills Bridge	38-17-01	17	4527620	688290	107

CLINTON COUNTY

Logan Mill Bridge	38-18-01	18	4541920	299300	108

COLUMBIA/NORTHUMBERLAND COUNTIES

Richards Bridge	38-19-01 38-49-07	18	4524920	372890	89
Krickbaum Bridge	38-19-32 38-49-12	18	4522700	372890	89
Lawrence L. Knoebel Bridge	38-19-39 38-49-13	18	4526140	373260	91

COLUMBIA COUNTY

Fowlersville Bridge	38-19-05	18	4545520	388440	91
Shoemaker Bridge	38-19-06	18	4556480	371080	91
Sam Eckman Bridge	38-19-08	18	4559320	374970	92
Josiah Hess Bridge	38-19-10	18	4552160	387520	93
East Paden Bridge	38-19-11	18	4551300	386050	93
West Paden Bridge	38-19-12	18	4551300	386050	94
Welle Hess, Laubach Bridge	38-19-13	18	4569120	384370	94
Snyder Bridge	38-19-14	18	4528520	382520	94
Wagner Bridge	38-19-15	18	4527500	384220	94
Davis Bridge	38-19-16	18	4529670	378720	95
Wanich Bridge	38-19-18	18	4544030	375300	95
Furnace Bridge	38-19-20	18	4529020	377020	95
Stillwater Bridge	38-19-21	18	4556290	385810	96
"Y" Bridge	38-19-22	18	4571600	385740	96
Kramer Bridge	38-19-23	18	4552970	379760	96

Jud Christian Bridge	38-19-25	18	4561340	376460	96
Patterson Bridge	38-19-26	18	4551660	380980	97
Parr's Mill Bridge	38-19-29	18	4529190	375940	98
Rohrbach Bridge	38-19-31	18	4528550	372640	99
Rupert Bridge	38-19-33	18	4537520	376080	99
Hollingshead Bridge	38-19-34	18	4534200	378140	99
Riegel Bridge	38-19-35	18	4529900	372520	99
Creasyville Bridge	38-19-36	18	4563110	377470	100
Johnson Bridge	38-19-37	18	4526050	374970	100

CUMBERLAND COUNTY

Thompson Bridge	38-21-10	18	4447780	390410	40
Ramp Bridge	38-21-11	18	4445720	284980	40
Bowmansdale Bridge	38-21-13	18	4446660	330400	41

DAUPHIN COUNTY

Everhart Bridge	38-22-02	18	4467150	337830	42
Henninger Farm Bridge	38-22-11	18	4493150	348980	43

ERIE COUNTY

Harrington Bridge	38-25-02	17	4635150	547375	121
Gudgeonville Bridge	38-25-03	17	4647800	560800	122
Waterford Bridge	38-25-04	17	4643560	585850	122
Carman Bridge	38-25-05	17	4640750	547200	122

FRANKLIN COUNTY

Martin's Mill Bridge	38-28-01	18	4405120	262200	44
Witherspoon Red Bridge	38-28-02	18	4407840	255530	45

GREENE COUNTY

Carmichaels Bridge	38-30-21	17	4416520	588980	8
Shriver Bridge	38-30-29	17	4411440	561650	9
King Bridge	38-30-24	17	4400840	562300	9
Lippincott Bridge	38-30-25	17	4421620	573640	10
Red, Neils Bridge	38-30-27	17	4407140	584400	10
Scott Bridge	38-30-28	17	4415280	557640	11
Grimes Bridge	38-30-22	17	4422840	571770	11
White Bridge	38-30-30	17	4406420	581120	12
Neddie Woods Bridge	38-30-26	17	4412620	565460	12

HUNTINGDON COUNTY

St. Mary's, Shade Gap Bridge	38-31-01	18	4454360	255030	13

INDIANA COUNTY

Dice's, Trussal Bridge	38-32-03	17	4510200	653300	14
Harmon's Bridge	38-32-04	17	4510620	654040	14
Kintersburg Bridge	38-32-06	17	4508510	662060	15
Thomas Ford Bridge	38-32-06	17	4502730	649040	15

JUNIATA COUNTY

Academia, Pomeroy Bridge	38-34-01	18	4485270	290460	45
Dimmsville Bridge	38-34-02	18	4497040	319040	45
Lehman's, Port Royal Bridge	38-34-04	18	4489040	297060	46

JUNIATA/SNYDER COUNTIES

North Oriental Bridge	38-34-05	18	4502970	329990	109
	38-55-05				

East Oriental Bridge	38-34-06	18	4500380	330760	110
	38-55-06				

LANCASTER/CHESTER COUNTIES

Mercer's Mill Bridge	38-36-38	18	4420390	416120	47
	38-15-19				
Pine Grove Bridge	38-36-41	18	4405150	410540	47
	38-15-22				

LANCASTER COUNTY

Pool Forge Bridge	38-36-01	18	4443660	414810	47
Weaver's Mill Bridge	38-36-02	18	4442390	416800	48
Kurtz's Mill Bridge	38-36-03	18	4429890	390640	49
Bitzer's Mill Bridge	38-36-04	18	4443750	401840	49
Pinetown, Bushong's Mill Bridge	38-36-05	18	4440020	393580	49
Erb's Bridge	38-36-34	18	4446890	394050	50
Red Run Mill Bridge	38-36-10	18	4447600	407870	50
Bucher's Mill Bridge	38-36-12	18	4451230	403420	51
Guy Bard's, Keller's Bridge	38-36-13	18	4447100	397380	51
Zook's Mill Bridge	38-36-14	18	4442760	395060	52
Buck Hill Bridge	38-36-15	18	4443010	389170	52
Landis Mill Bridge	38-36-16	18	4436010	385270	52
White Rock Bridge	38-36-18	18	4408650	406700	52
Leaman Place Bridge	38-36-20	18	4429480	405410	53
Herr's Mill Bridge	38-36-21	18	4429280	400800	54
Neff's Mill Bridge	38-36-22	18	4425900	395320	54
Lime Valley Bridge	38-36-23	18	4423900	394520	54
Baumgardner's Mill Bridge	38-36-25	18	4420640	389300	54
Colemanville Bridge	38-36-26	18	4417160	385250	55
Forry's Mill Bridge	38-36-28	18	4435960	373920	55
Schenck's Mill Bridge	38-36-30	18	4441360	378520	55
Shearer's Bridge	38-36-31	18	4447560	381620	56
Kaufman's Distillery Bridge	38-36-32	18	4444940	379880	56
Jackson's Mill Bridge	38-36-33	18	4416630	407620	57
Hunsecker's Mill Bridge	38-36-06	18	4437980	393600	57
Risser's Mill Bridge	38-36-36	18	4444110	371760	57
Seigrist's Mill Bridge	38-36-37	18	4437010	374540	57
Willow Hill Bridge	38-36-43	18	4430940	397440	58

LAWRENCE COUNTY

McConnell's Mill Bridge	38-37-01	17	4533640	569820	123
Banks Bridge	38-37-02	17	4548840	559960	124

LEHIGH COUNTY

Bogerts Bridge	38-39-01	18	4490800	457280	80
Wehr's Bridge	38-39-02	18	4497540	451780	80
Manasses Guth Bridge	38-39-03	18	4497440	453170	83
Rex's Bridge	38-39-04	18	4498180	448160	83
Geiger's Bridge	38-39-05	18	4499460	447850	83
Schlicher's Bridge	38-39-06	18	4501170	446980	83

LUZERNE COUNTY

Bittenbender's Bridge	38-40-01	18	4559340	397260	100

LYCOMING COUNTY

Buttonwood Bridge	38-41-01	18	4597320	322200	110
Cogan House Bridge	38-41-02	18	4585080	316000	110
Lairdsville Bridge	38-41-03	18	4562840	362830	112

MERCER COUNTY

Kidd's Mill Bridge	38-43-01	18	4577960	550360	125

MONTOUR/NORTHUMBERLAND COUNTIES

Gottlieb Brown Bridge	38-49-01	18	4540260	350800	102

MONTOUR COUNTY

Keefer Bridge	38-47-03	18	4543590	357780	103

NORTHAMPTON COUNTY

Kreidersville Bridge	38-48-01	18	4507980	458360	84

NORTHUMBERLAND COUNTY

Keefer Station Bridge	38-49-02	18	4525600	354750	112
Rishel Bridge	38-49-05	18	4533710	347170	112
Himmel's Church Bridge	38-49-06	18	4509230	354140	114

PERRY COUNTY

Bistline Bridge	38-50-03	18	4467540	290120	58
Adairs, Cisna Mill Bridge	38-50-04	18	4468260	394100	58
Red Bridge	38-50-06	18	4492520	330360	58
Saville Bridge	38-50-07	18	4478920	296740	59
Kochendefer Bridge	38-50-09	18	4477370	297460	59
Rice, Landisburg Bridge	38-50-10	18	4467380	303810	60
New Germantown Bridge	38-50-11	18	4464740	281740	60
Mt. Pleasant Bridge	38-50-12	18	4465620	283700	61
Book's, Kaufman Bridge	38-50-13	18	4466620	285500	61
Enslow, Turkey Tail Bridge	38-50-14	18	4467380	287280	62
Waggoner Mill Bridge	38-50-15	18	4470140	298480	62
Dellville Bridge	38-50-16	18	4470050	320280	63
Fleisher Bridge	38-50-17	18	4484110	317060	64
Clays Bridge	38-50-18	18	4480580	316060	64

PHILADELPHIA COUNTY

Thomas Mill Bridge	38-51-01	18	4435520	480740	85

SCHUYLKILL COUNTY

Zimmerman's Bridge	38-54-01	18	4488800	387720	64
Rock Bridge	38-54-02	18	4488860	390320	64

SNYDER COUNTY

Dreese's, Beavertown Bridge	38-55-02	18	4515840	318940	115
Klinepeter's, Gross Bridge	38-55-03	18	4513380	312300	116
Aline, Meiserville Bridge	38-55-04	18	4504520	332700	116

SOMERSET COUNTY

Beechdale Bridge	38-56-01	17	4416260	668060	16
Packsaddle Bridge	38-56-02	17	4415140	686670	16
Barronvale Bridge	38-56-03	17	4423730	647730	17
Walter's Mill Bridge	38-56-05	17	4436600	663940	17
King's Bridge	38-56-06	17	4422050	647690	19
Glessner Bridge	38-56-08	17	4432500	677400	19

New Baltimore Bridge	38-56-09	17	4428470	690200	21
Trostletown Bridge	38-56-10	17	4440220	675120	21
Shaffer's Bridge	38-56-11	17	4460740	673060	21
Lower Humbert Bridge	38-56-12	17	4411160	643470	21

SULLIVAN COUNTY
Forksville Bridge	38-57-01	18	4594000	366420	104
Hillsgrove Bridge	38-57-02	18	4591040	360440	104
Sonestown Bridge	38-57-03	18	4578160	369880	105

UNION COUNTY
Millmont Red Bridge	38-60-01	18	4527260	318350	117
Hayes Bridge	38-60-02	18	4532460	323840	117
Hassenplug Bridge	38-60-03	18	4523100	327370	118
Factory, Horsham Bridge...............	38-60-04	18	4548460	340100	118
Lewisburg Penitentiary Bridge	38-60-05	18	(Not available)		119

WASHINGTON/GREENE COUNTIES
Davis, Horn, Overholtzer Bridge	38-30-31	17	4428860	580020	22
	38-63-31				

WASHINGTON COUNTY
Sprowl's Bridge	38-63-03	17	4428910	550610	23
Bailey Bridge	38-63-08	17	4430140	568630	23
Brownlee, Scott Bridge.................	38-63-09	17	4432600	551360	24
Crawford Bridge.......................	38-63-10	17	4427940	545040	24
Danley Bridge	38-63-11	17	4433810	547800	24
Day Bridge............................	38-63-12	17	4431060	560320	24
Devil's Den, McClurg Bridge	38-63-13	17	4474800	541840	25
Ebenezer Bridge	38-63-14	17	4449200	581630	25
Erskine Bridge........................	38-63-15	17	4435020	541240	26
Henry Bridge..........................	38-63-16	17	4450470	583670	26
Hughes Bridge.........................	38-63-17	17	4431560	571650	26
Jackson's Mill Bridge	38-63-18	17	4474730	543300	26
Krepps Bridge	38-63-19	17	4465570	556790	27
Leatherman Bridge.....................	38-63-20	17	4440080	579120	27
Lyle Bridge	38-63-21	17	4478060	553740	28
Longdon L. Miller Bridge	38-63-22	17	4427580	545000	28
Mays, Blaney Bridge....................	38-63-23	17	4437450	543680	28
Martin's Mill Bridge	38-63-24	17	4429420	574110	28
Plant's Bridge	38-63-26	17	4430040	549820	29
Ralston Freeman Bridge.................	38-63-27	17	4477260	541790	29
Wilson's Mill Bridge	38-63-28	17	4455940	551140	30
Wyit Sprowls Bridge....................	38-63-29	17	4428940	545850	30
Wright, Cerl Bridge	38-63-30	17	4445630	581000	31
Sawhill Bridge........................	38-63-34	17	4447700	549690	31
Pine Bank Bridge......................	38-63-35	17	4459740	543270	31

WESTMORELAND COUNTY
Bells Mills Bridge	38-65-01	17	4452660	609740	32